A Blazing Star
The Founding of the Thirteen Colonies

A Blazing Star

The Founding of the Thirteen Colonies

by Earl Schenck Miers

RAND McNALLY & COMPANY
Chicago   New York   San Francisco

Cover illustration reprinted by courtesy of
William L. Clements Library
University of Michigan

CONTENTS

A Blazing Star

The Founding of the Thirteen Colonies

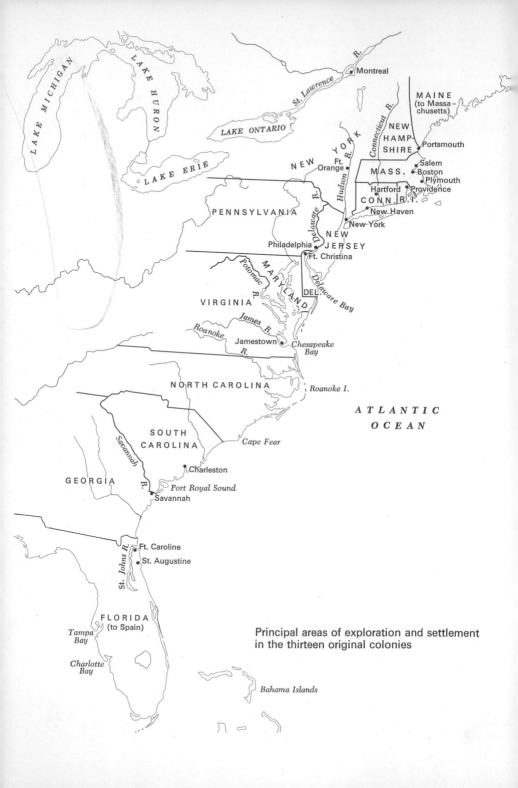

Principal areas of exploration and settlement in the thirteen original colonies

Chapter 1

FOR FORTUNE AND FREEDOM
A Game for Historical Detectives

The crew who had sailed with Christopher Columbus
aboard three caravels as the sun rose over the little port
of Palos on August 3, 1492, within two months verged on
mutiny. There had been no indication of bad feeling
when Columbus refitted his ships at the Canary Islands.
In an optimistic mood Columbus had estimated the remaining voyage to Japan and the East Indies at only
2,400 miles. Indeed, his sailors had talked gaily among

themselves over who would first sight land and claim a princely reward of 10,000 Spanish *maravedis*.

But since then weeks had passed with only the sight of one green wave rolling after another. Faces grew sullen and nerves frayed. Nothing but ocean and stars, ocean and stars—how long could a man endure this without going insane? Defiance brought sulky obedience when orders were issued.

Mates, sensing the truth, faced Columbus with the stark and bitter danger of an impending rebellion. The admiral smiled cheerily on this Wednesday, October 10, as his mates confronted him. Why should anyone be downcast when in a day and night they were sailing 59 leagues, or the equivalent of 177 land miles? They should continue sailing toward the west, resting their faith in God.

That night Columbus sent hurriedly for the two royal representatives who had sailed with him—Pedro Gutierrez, a gentleman of the king's bedchamber, and Rodrigo Sanchez, inspector of the fleet.

"I think I saw a light," Columbus said, describing it as resembling the fluttering of a wax candle.

Aboard the pitching deck of the *Pinta*, as the caravel dipped first toward the ocean's bottom, then rose toward the moon and stars, Columbus's officially appointed companions strained their eyes. Yes, Columbus was right, Gutierrez said—there was a light. Sanchez would not agree. Next morning, as Columbus shifted his course to west-southwest, signs of land increased. Sandpipers were seen, and green reeds and a small branch covered with berries appeared in the water. Suddenly a sailor, Rodrigo de Triana, shouted:

"Land ahoy!"

The following day, Friday, October 12, Columbus stepped into the New World on the soil of an island the Indians called Guanahani (Watling Island in the Bahamas). He kissed the ground and praised God; then, flanked by Gutierrez and Sanchez, he planted a standard bearing an "F" for Ferdinand and a "Y" for Ysabel, king and queen of Spain, sponsors of the expedition. Members of the crew, who just days ago had spoken of mutiny, cheered wildly as their admiral renamed the island San Salvador. Columbus was delighted by the good-humored, intelligent natives, whom he believed would make good Christians.

Thus began a race among four principal nationalities —the Spanish, French, English, and Dutch—to plant new empires across the sea. To unravel the process by which colonies were founded along the Atlantic coast as forerunners of our present great nation may be one of the most fascinating problems in historical detection. Even authorities do not always agree on the course and dates of events, since the original, ancient texts they use often are at considerable variance. A good example is the first landing of the Spanish in Florida: Some say it was north of present-day Saint Augustine, and others that it was 175 miles to the south. Whether Santo Domingo is called Española or Hispaniola depends on whether one uses the Spanish or Indian name for the island. But irritating though these discrepancies may be, they fade into the background as the full mystery begins to untangle.

In that age of superstition when many still believed the world was flat, the intelligence of Columbus's achievement raced like prairie fire across Europe, and within four years England was pushing her toe into the door of an overseas empire with the voyages of John and Sebastian Cabot. France's challenge came more than half a century later and was marked by almost immediate violence.

Spain at least was always consistent. She came with sword and cross, seeking plunder and Catholic converts, and she had small patience with French Huguenots or English Pilgrims who sniveled over their need for religious freedom. If the shoe were on the other foot, said the Spaniards, see how quickly the situation would change—as indeed it did with the Pilgrims in Massachusetts.

But this observation races ahead of our story. Long before Columbus stumbled unwittingly upon the New World, the folklore of the Old World was filled with legends of others who had been to a land of astonishing mystery. North America was inhabited as far back as 35,000 to 18,000 B.C., probably by Asiatic peoples. But did the Phoenicians touch the shores of New Hampshire sometime between 480 and 146 B.C.? In A.D. 64 did the Romans so terrify a band of early Christians that they sought refuge in or near present-day Virginia? Or did Hoei-Shin, a Chinese, set out some four hundred

years later in search of the "Painted People"? Did an
Irish monk first behold the beauty of Florida in A.D. 551?
Perhaps the voyages of Leif Ericsson (A.D. 1003) and
Thorvald Ericsson (A.D. 1007) to that country they
called Vinland actually occurred, as we believe; but
were they influenced by Bjarni Herjulfsson, another
Viking, who reputedly beheld America in A.D. 986 and
was so disgusted with sailing so far off course that he
neither landed ncr divulged the nature of his mistake for
the next sixteen years?

Legends did not always die quickly in the Old
World, although they were often revised to suit the
needs of later generations. Perhaps Prester John really
existed and began the rumor of the *Fons Juventutis,* or
Fountain of Youth, as early as the twelfth century. No
one knew for certain whether the fabulous kingdom he
ruled was in Asia or Africa, where, according to the
Encyclopaedia Britannica, "there were no poor in his
dominions, no thief or robber, no flatterer or miser, no
dissensions, no lies and no vices." Streams teemed with
fish, the sands with gems, and there was a "Fountain of
Youth, the pebbles of which give light, restore sight and
render the possessor invisible." Marco Polo believed that
the descendants of Prester John lived on the plain of
Kuku Khotan, about three hundred miles northwest of
Peking.

The legend altered again when a Sir John Mandeville
claimed to have found the *Fons Juventutis* at a place
called Polombe where, Mandeville declared, he "drank
thereof thrice" and "feel me the better and the haler." In

1511 the legend was still being repeated in Spain, although the location of the fountain now was situated on the island of Bimini, somewhere north of Santo Domingo.

Thus are wild tales and lies often woven into the fabric of history.

Chapter 2

HIGH STAKES
Spain Seeks to Steal a Continent

Although the man's hair was snow-white and lines on his face revealed the hard life he had led, Juan Ponce de León in 1511 still could not bear the thought of growing old. A warrior of distinction against the Moors, a companion of Christopher Columbus on his second voyage to the New World, Ponce de León had been conspicuous in the subjugation of Santo Domingo (Hispaniola) and was appointed governor of Puerto Rico, as became his noble Castilian lineage.

Juan Ponce cared little for the honors that had come to him. What did they mean to a man of energy still ambitious to seek a fortune and to recover his youth? With glowing eyes, he listened to the tales natives related of a spring on one of the nearby islands of the West Indies. Anyone who bathed in the waters of this spring, Ponce de León heard, would gain eternal youth and everlasting beauty. On this magical island golden apples grew. Rare tropical flowers perfumed the air. Delicious fruits were served by handsome maidens.

Nightly Juan Ponce dreamed of this fountain of youth. Tossing in bed, he felt driven to discover it. In the spring of 1512 he fitted ships at his own expense for a voyage to the fabulous land the natives described. He sailed through the Bahamas from island to island, tasting the water and swimming in every lake and stream he could find, but the miracle of revival did not occur. A new year began.

Undaunted, Juan Ponce sailed off in a northwesterly direction. Soon the air *was* scented with flowers. The old cavalier could not keep the joy from his eyes. He turned west toward the perfumed fragrance and soon came upon a long stretch of wooded coast. Magnolia blossoms gave beauty to the forest.

On a morning in April, Juan Ponce and his crew landed near the site of present-day Saint Augustine, destined to become the oldest city in the continental United States. A hymn was sung in honor of Jesus, after which Juan Ponce took possession of the domain in the name of the sovereign of Castile. Ponce first sighted the land on Easter Sunday (*Pascua florida*), and so named the area that was to become our southernmost Atlantic state, Florida. He did not at this time realize it was connected to the North American continent.

A search of the coastal forests and savannas yielded no fountain of youth. By now Ponce must have been downcast if not disheartened. He sailed southward, bucked the Gulf Stream, and doubled the Florida keys. Presently he discovered a group of small islands that he named the Dry Tortugas, after the turtles abounding there, and explored other islands in Charlotte Bay along the west coast of Florida.

Sailing back to the West Indies, Ponce met a wrinkled old woman who lived as a hermitess on an island of the Bahamas. Ponce must not lose faith in the existence of the fountain of youth, she declared, for it existed at a place known as Bimini (the same island Ponce had heard mentioned in Spain two years before).

Ponce took the woman with him. The seas were stormy, and the governor felt the aches of increasing age as he returned to his base at Puerto Rico. Gradually Ponce began to believe his hair must remain white. He returned to Spain, reported his discovery of Florida, and asked that he be made governor of the colony that should be planted there.

Many years passed, however, before the colonization was attempted. A vicious battle was fought with the Caribs, hostile Indians in this land of many islands like Santo Domingo, and Ponce was lucky to escape with his life. Finally, however, Ponce could resume his voyage to

Florida, which he now suspected was part of a continent. Filled with dreams of becoming as wealthy as Hernando Cortés had in Mexico, Ponce loaded two ships and departed from Puerto Rico in 1521, struck the west coast of Florida, passed Charlotte Bay, and probably disembarked about sixty miles northward near the site of present-day Tampa.

The reception given the Spaniards was hardly cordial. Enraged by Spanish slave raids along this coast, Indians with bows and arrows and long pikes stormed out of the forest. War whoops reverberated through the trees. Arrows filled the air. The Spaniards fell. Juan Ponce, severely wounded in the thigh, reached Cuba, where he had left his wife and son, before he died. Upon his tomb the Latin inscription read:

IN THIS SEPULCHRE REST THE BONES OF A MAN WHO WAS
LION BY NAME AND STILL MORE BY NATURE

As the years passed, much blood would be spilled in Florida between red men and white, and also between French and Spaniards, for possession of the New World. True, England had established a strong claim when Henry VII, the first of the Tudor dynasty that would end with Queen Elizabeth I, dispatched an expedition from Bristol under the command of a Venetian merchant, John Cabot, four years after Columbus had unwittingly found the New World. Cabot could have five ships and as many seamen as he wished, just so he paid for them—Henry VII liked to clutch his shillings. The king's charter permitted Cabot "to discover and occupy isles or countries of the heathen or infidels before unknown to Christians, accounting to the king for a fifth part of the profit upon their return to the port of Bristol." Commonly, in this age, Christians believed that they owned all lands inhabited by "pagans." John Cabot, however, may have died in 1498 and perhaps never took part in an expedition, but his twenty-one-year-old son, Sebastian, kept alive Henry VII's wavering interest in exploration.

Sebastian liked geography and navigation. "When my father died," he said, "in that time when news was brought that Don Christopher Colonus [Columbus], Genoese, had discovered the coast of India, whereof there was great talk in all the court of King Henry the Seventh . . . insomuch that all men with great admiration affirmed it to be a thing more divine than human, to sail by the west into the east where spices grew. . . ." Sebastian sailed off in two caravels, supplied by the king, but what he accomplished was dubious. Whether he discovered Newfoundland or the coast of Labrador, historians dispute. Likely he touched the shore of Maine and may have gone as far south as the Carolinas. His maps were fine, at any rate. Sebastian, however, did not impress Henry VII, who was preoccupied with problems at home. The first of the Tudors fell into a kind of stupefied indifference toward the New World.

Actually, no one understood better than the Spaniards the high stakes involved in the discovery of the Americas and the West Indies. Soon a tremendous fortune in gold and silver was entering Spain from the Indies, and Spain had no intention of losing this revenue.

Publication of all maps and navigational charts that could aid in discovering this source of wealth was forbidden. Foreigners could not be hired as sailors aboard any ships that were bound for the West Indies. Masters of vessels were required to be natives of Navarre, Aragon, or Castile.

The Spaniards were astute enough to realize that their enemies would find a way around these restrictions. The French ambassador at Madrid had his sources for learning quickly when a Spanish "treasure fleet" had departed from Peru and Mexico. The French banks at Lyons also employed spies. The Portuguese offered to bribe Spanish pilots. In Seville, French pilots hid among the crews of departing Spanish ships.

But Spain was wily in outwitting her enemies. A commercial company, formed in Haiti to raid the country for gold and slaves, was headed by Lucas Vásquez de Ayllón, an athletic fellow, good-looking, and possessing enormous wealth from the pearl divers and mines he owned in the West Indies. But there was a deep streak of cruelty in Ayllón, who had all but exterminated the island natives working as slaves in his mines.

(The extent of slavery in the West Indies is little realized today. By 1560 the French estimated that in Puerto Rico there were 15,000 Negroes and less than 500 Spaniards; Hispaniola contained approximately 2,000 Spaniards and more than 30,000 Negroes; and along the coast of Venezuela the blacks outnumbered the whites twenty to one.)

Eager to replenish the slaves in his mines, Ayllón sailed in two ships in 1520, coasting along North America as far as South Carolina, where he entered St. Helena Sound. The Indians crowded the shore, believing that they beheld sea monsters. Ayllón persuaded the natives that his men came only as friends. Invited aboard the vessels, the Indians were feasted and virtually soaked with strong wine until they became drunk and stupid, whereupon they were thrown into the hold as Ayllón's first captives.

Six years later Ayllón returned and sailed into Port Royal Sound, where the natives of Chicora (as South Carolina was then called) warmly greeted him and his comrades near the present site of Beaufort. The foundation of a town was planned, but the Spaniards never forgot their real purpose for being there. About two hundred Indians were invited aboard the two ships for a feast that lasted two or three days. This time, however, the Indians turned the tables and massacred their "benefactors." A few Spaniards escaped, among them Ayllón, who soon died of the wounds he received. Another expedition, under Alonso de Ojeda, a navigator, encountered a similar slaughter. News of the true character of the white man was carried through the forests by Indian couriers.

These years were of tremendous importance. A month after Ponce de León left Puerto Rico in the spring of 1512, death came to the famous Italian navigator Amerigo

Vespucci, who made four voyages to the New World, gave his name to two continents, and became convinced that America was not part of Asia. This last fact the Spaniards steadfastly refused to believe, calling all the unknown land north of Mexico "Florida." North America, they insisted, must be a peninsula of Asia.

Within the first three decades of the sixteenth century, however, Spanish knowledge of the New World advanced enormously. Crossing Panama in 1513, Vasco Núñez de Balboa discovered the Pacific Ocean. Mexico had been conquered and looted by 1521; from 1519 to 1521 Ferdinand Magellan circumnavigated the world; Peru was conquered by Francisco Pizarro in another eleven years, and Spanish vessels had sailed the North American coast from Florida to Newfoundland, as well as exploring the Gulf of Mexico. Inland the Spaniards traveled the soil that would become Texas, and may have marched as far north as Oklahoma. The fabulous treasures from these new territories did not come too soon to Spain, bankrupt after six hundred years of war against the Moors.

The age was also one of mystery and superstition. Stories were told of a mythical island in the Atlantic named Antilla, to which seven priests had sailed when the Moors conquered Spain. The priests had built, these tales said, the Seven Cities of Antilla, where gold paved the streets as a sign of their incredible riches. Other rumors placed these cities of gold somewhere on the North American mainland, calling them the Seven Cities of Cíbola.

The source of the latter stories was Álvar Núñez Cabeza De Vaca, whose ships and crew of 250 were wrecked by a hurricane in the Gulf of Mexico in 1528. De Vaca waded out of the stormy waters onto Galveston Island, where he was enslaved by the Indians. In less than a year De Vaca escaped into the interior of Texas, and five years after the shipwreck caught up with three other survivors of his fleet who were wandering along the Colorado River near the Texas coast. Two were Spaniards, the third a Moorish slave.

Strange tales sprang up among the Indians about Stephen, the slave. So great were this Moor's powers of magic, the red men believed, that they had only to touch his cloak for their wounds to heal and their illnesses to vanish. Protected by this superstition, De Vaca's party traveled west through mesquite country until they crossed the Pecos River; then some distance from present-day El Paso they forded the Rio Grande. Meanwhile, Stephen increased his powers by learning how to communicate with the Indians in their own language. Everywhere he was showered with gifts of beads, buffalo skins, and pouches of pearls.

As the first Europeans to visit New Mexico and Arizona, De Vaca's party found Indians who lived in permanent homes and ate beans, squashes, and corn. Here the wanderers heard stories of rich cities in a northland called Cíbola, where even the arrowheads sparkled like emeralds. Eight years after their disaster in the Gulf of Mexico, De Vaca and his friends were rescued by a party of slave hunters. Excitedly all discussed the Cities of

Cíbola, unable to realize, of course, that they described no more than the light of the sun shining upon the pueblos, or cliff-cities, of the Zuñi Indians.

Meanwhile, the fable of the Cities of Gold excited Hernando De Soto, who had fought with Pizarro in Peru. De Soto dreamed of wealth, as all influential Spaniards did in that age. In the spring of 1539 De Soto left Havana with 570 men and nine ships, finally reaching Charlotte Bay on the western coast of Florida. Here, in high spirits, he landed his armored soldiers and knights, two hundred horses, and one hundred hogs.

Two years of nightmare followed. As De Soto plunged through the wilderness of Florida, Alabama, the Carolinas, and Tennessee, this vainglorious leader was almost constantly at war with the Indians. Hunger and sickness were rife among his troops. A sorrowful group they made, wearing raccoon and wildcat skins under their rusted armor, when in April or May of 1541 De Soto stumbled upon the mighty Mississippi.

The likely place of discovery was some thirty or thirty-five miles below present-day Memphis, where the river was a mile wide. In hollowed-out logs the Spaniards, on June 29, 1541, sailed southward and landed in Arkansas near Sunflower Landing, south of Helena. They had found the stream swift and deep, filled with much fallen timber that rocked them around, and many kinds of strange fish. They later crossed the Arkansas River and discovered a "very warm and brackish lake" where Hot Springs now stands.

De Soto looked upon the Indians as fools and did not

trouble to conceal his feelings. He told the red men that he was a god and, showing them a mirror, said it revealed to him everything they did and thought. Wisely the Indians rid themselves of their invaders by declaring the gold they sought was in some other distant place. The Spaniards wintered along the Ouachita River, living on corn, beans, pecans, and dried persimmons begged from the Indians.

When spring came, malaria swept their encampment. Each day, it seemed, another Spaniard passed away. Then De Soto himself lay burning with fever, and when he died, the Spaniards shuddered at how the Indians might react to the death of a self-styled god. For three days they hid De Soto's corpse, until they decided one night to bury it in the sandy bottom of the Mississippi. They told the Indians that De Soto and some of his comrades had returned to heaven on a visit.

The deaths of Ponce de León, Ayllón, and De Soto were saddening, but when Spain realized how much wealth was pouring into her treasury, her grief quickly disappeared. By decree of Pope Alexander VI, Spain had claimed all of South America except Brazil, and the northern continent at least as far as Newfoundland. By 1561 the *Armada de las Carreras de las Indias* was organized to protect Spanish war vessels and the merchantmen from the pirates of other nations inclined to attack her "treasure fleets." But Spain's neighbors well knew of her prosperity and hungered to share in it. France was the first to enter this race for riches when in 1535 Jacques

Cartier sailed up the Saint Lawrence River, but other factors were astir that would heighten this rivalry.

The Era of Reformation, when Protestants led by Martin Luther challenged the authority of the Pope of Rome, was sweeping across Europe, bringing bitter civil dissension and religious wars. The impact of this developing struggle would have sharp repercussions in colonial America.

Chapter 3

FORT CAROLINE
France vs. Spain in the New World

Catherine, as the Regent of France, watched her young son romping with his favorite Italian greyhound. To his mother this ninth King Charles, not yet in his teens in 1560, was already a handsome young rascal in his suit of royal purple velvet. Catherine, a Medici, combined the brilliance and cupidity of mind that distinguished this Italian family of kings and popes.

Plots within the court were a common pastime to

Catherine. When it was suggested by distinguished Protestant leaders that France's Huguenots, or Protestants,
should be allowed their religious freedom by colonizing
in Florida, Catherine quickly agreed. What could aid the
future Charles IX more than to free him from France's
growing number of hardheaded Huguenots? Catherine
said, gladly and emphatically, Let the Protestants go!

There is wide doubt over whether two ships or six
carried the first Huguenots to the New World. All
authorities agree, however, that in selecting as leader of
the expedition Jean Ribaut, an experienced mariner of
Dieppe, a brave man was honored. Moreover, Ribaut
was devoted to Catherine's policy of never yielding to
Spain the freedom of the seas any quicker than France
should "consent to be deprived of . . . the heavens."

Through the bluster and downpours of an Atlantic
winter, Ribaut led his fleet in 1562 across the gale-tossed
waves and by April was sailing along the "sweet-smelling
coasts" of Florida north of the future site of Saint Augustine. Grapevines festooned the trees. The wings of birds
made bright flashes against the forest background. Entering the Saint Johns River, Ribaut marveled at the
number of silkworms on the boughs of the mulberry
trees. The Indians were gently inclined, their land not
yet "broken with plough irons." In this seeming paradise
the French paused just long enough to thank God for
their safe voyage and to claim the territory in the name
of Charles IX.

Again Ribaut sailed north until he reached Port
Royal Sound (South Carolina). For reasons never ex-

plained, he considered Port Royal Island ideal for a colony. Here he landed his little group of thirty persons. Although the Indians appeared friendly, he supervised the construction of a fort. "Let each love God and his neighbor," Ribaut advised the settlers before he returned to France for additional supplies and colonists. Unhappily, he found his homeland torn by civil war between Catholics and Huguenots, and Catherine turned deaf ears to Ribaut's pleas for help.

Naturally the colonists on Port Royal Island could not know these facts. Awaiting the return of Ribaut, they did not cultivate their lands. Days stretched into weeks and then into months, and still there was no sight of Ribaut. The Huguenots begged corn from the Indians, but their harvests had been sparse. It would make better sense, the red men said, if the French sought aid from the more bounteously provisioned tribes to the south.

This advice proved very wise. In a little pinnace that the Huguenots may have fashioned for themselves they journeyed to an Indian village on the Savannah River. The chief, or king, Ouadé, was a man of unusual grace and intelligence. The walls of the dwelling in which he entertained his white visitors were decorated with tapestries. Good-humoredly he loaded the little pinnace with corn and beans.

But bad luck seemed to stick like swamp flies on these first Huguenots in America. Hardly had they returned to Port Royal Island than their fort burned. When Ouadé heard this news, he sent another pinnace filled with corn, beans, and squashes. Yet the worst misfortune to bedevil the settlers arose from Ribaut's appointment of Capt. Albert de la Pierria as their governor.

One might have to travel a continent to find a more vicious, intemperate man than Pierria. He hanged whomever he pleased for whatever reason he pleased. A soldier who had angered him he doomed to starvation on a deserted island. Dissension swept Port Royal Island and Pierria responded with disciplinary measures that grew ever harsher. Seeds of mutiny were deeply planted.

The Huguenots selected Nicholas Barré to lead an uprising that ended in Pierria's death. But with grim famine facing them once more, they tottered around in growing discontent, until finally they constructed a frail brigantine and sailed for home. One disaster followed another. First, they were so long becalmed that their dwindling provisions once more threatened starvation. Then a wild tempest shook their homemade brigantine like a child's boat fashioned from paper and twigs. They ate their shoes and leather doublets, and some died of hunger, while only a miracle kept afloat a craft half filled with water. They were about to cast lots to determine who should be slaughtered to make food for the others when a wavering cry sounded: "Land!"

So their odyssey of miracles endured. Not only did they sight a green shore, but a British vessel soon appeared and rescued them. Among its crew was a Frenchman who had sailed with Ribaut and recognized the settlers. He gave them food and drink and satisfied another craving with news of home and friends.

England was then at war with France, and these Huguenots presented quite a problem. Many of the survivors were landed at La Coruña in Spain, where they were told to make their way home as best they could. Those known to have engaged in the mutinous murder of Pierria were carried to England, where they were tried and imprisoned.

Spain—also at war with France—had no intention of ignoring this French intrusion into territory they claimed. As May was fading in 1564, an expedition of twenty-five men under Don Hernando de Manrique de Rojas left the West Indies. His frigate, *Nuestra Señora de la Concepción,* sighted the Florida coast at Cape Canaveral. Manrique was no wild-eyed explorer and he proceeded cautiously northward along the coast as though believing the earth might be flat, after all. He would only sail by daylight. But the discovery of a wooden box bearing sacred objects confirmed the fact that he was on the right course.

Finally Manrique found the remains of Ribaut's colony on Port Royal Island. More surprising was the presence of Guillaume Rufin, a seventeen-year-old boy who, not wishing to trust his life to the complete navigational ignorance of his fellow Huguenots, had escaped from the colony. Dressed in the clothes of the Indians who had cared for him, Rufin told De Rojas the tale of the distress that had befallen Ribaut's Huguenots. A wobbly, thatched hut of the French that still stood Manrique ordered burned to the ground. The standard claiming the land for Charles IX was found on its grassy knoll and carried away. Guillaume Rufin was transported to Cuba as a prisoner.

France was willing to try a second time to plant a colony in Florida. René de Laudonnière, a skilled marine officer and former companion of Ribaut, was selected to lead this expedition. Laudonnière was described as firm in mind and character, yet his previous experience in Florida served him little.

Three hundred colonists assembled for this second expedition. Of these, 110 were soldiers, and 120 were sailors. The others were certainly a miscellaneous lot: four women, including a housekeeper and chambermaid to Laudonnière; noblemen; an artist, Jacques Le Moyne de Morgues, who would supply some of the finest pictures ever drawn of the natives and region; an apothecary; an artificer (craftsman); a few foreigners; carpenters. Who were missing became equally important: clergymen, farmers, and field hands. Huguenots were in the majority, but some Roman Catholics were present.

Three vessels—the *Isabella*, sixty tons; the *Little Briton*, eighty tons; and the *Faulcon*, a man-of-war of three hundred tons—made the voyage. "The Queen," wrote Laudonnière, "has charged me very expressly to do no kind of wrong to the King of Spain's subjects, nor anything whereof he might conceive any jealousy"—a somewhat strange statement since Laudonnière was headed straight for the coast of Florida.

The fleet left Le Havre in April of 1564 and by late

June was in the vicinity of Saint Augustine. The sweetness of the air lured the men forward, and they reconnoitered the harbor the natives called Seploy and which Laudonnière renamed the River of Dolphins. Another two days led him to the River of May, or the Saint Johns, where he met Saturiba, an Indian chief who had known Ribaut. The chief led him to the pillar of conquest the Frenchman had erected in 1562, which the natives "kissed . . . with great reverence and besought us to do the like."

While Laudonnière rested on Saint Johns Bluff, beneath its palms and "cedars red as blood," he sent his lieutenant, Ottigny, to explore the interior. A rather wide-eyed Ottigny returned with a tale of having found people who had lived to ages of 250 and 350 years, but with considerably less Gallic romanticism Laudonnière commented drily: "They were the greatest thieves on earth, for they steal as well with the feet as with the hands." Laudonnière was pleased with the place, however, and ordered Fort Caroline built at a point where swamps, a creek, and a river prevented attack from the sea. From a wedge of silver Saturiba had given him, the Frenchman judged that precious metals must be close by.

Laudonnière had settled among the Timucua Indians, whose territories stretched as far south as Lake Miami. The artist Le Moyne, far better than Laudonnière, described the aborigines of this part of the New World. They were a finely proportioned people, Le Moyne said, and they tatooed their somewhat olive-hued bodies by pricking their skins with thorns and inserting an herb of an indelible color. The process was difficult, and often the Indians were sick for seven or eight days afterward. As protection against the sun's heat and at religious ceremonies, they rubbed their naked bodies with oil, a fact to which they ascribed their darkened skins, for they were far lighter at birth. Their hair was long and trussed up on their heads; their loincloths were made of deer hide; and they claimed remarkable powers of smell.

Warriors went to battle in a headdress of feathers, leaves, and grasses, or covered their heads with the skins of wild animals. Their faces were painted in fierce colors, and small disks of gold and silver hung by a chain at their chests.

The women were much fairer of complexion and, like the men, allowed the nails of their hands and feet to grow long so that they could be used to rip the flesh of an enemy. Inflated bladders of a small fish, dyed red, were forced through punctures in their ear lobes. Women lived apart from their husbands during pregnancy; and when a husband died or was killed, his wife had to cut her hair short and wait until it had grown to shoulder length before she could remarry.

Le Moyne was fascinated by Indian cures for the sick. Sometimes they were turned face downward over a bed of hot coals on which seeds were spread; the smoke made the Indians vomit as, supposedly, it entered all parts of the body. Tobacco in a pipe produced a similar result. Bleeding was another primitive remedy and was caused by slashing the forehead with the sharp edge of a shell.

The Timucuas lived in small villages. They planted corn in March and June, cultivating it with a hoe made from a fishbone fastened to a pole. In winter they retired to the forests, where they subsisted under shelters of palm leaves. During these cold months the Indians ate acorns, oysters, terrapin, deer (which they captured by disguising themselves within a deerskin), other game, fish, dogs, and snakes; and Laudonnière accused them of "putting sand into the pottage which they make of [corn] meal."

Since this was also alligator country, the Indians kept watch from a small hut near the river. The alligator is a noisy reptile when hunger drives it ashore, and its roars can be heard for quite a distance. The Indians came with long poles which they thrust down the alligator's throat. Then they turned the reptile onto its scaly back. With the soft belly now exposed, the alligator was killed with arrows and clubs.

Laudonnière declared that Saturiba's people possessed "no knowledge of God, nor of any religion, saving that which they see, as the Sun and the Moon." Occasionally human sacrifice was practiced. The Timucuas were believers in witchcraft. To prevent sickness, one drank out of another's cup after eating bear meat. A hooting owl brought luck and should never be disturbed. Either eating the right herbs or dyeing her palm-leaf hat with certain vegetables would bring a woman the man she loved. A bodily tremor indicated either someone's arrival or that some event would soon occur. All enemies were scalped with slips of reeds "sharper than any steel blade." Under attack of a war party, the women and children were always spared and brought back alive.

Had Laudonnière's colony behaved itself, it might well have survived. But the Frenchmen kept delaying their promise of supporting Saturiba against his enemies. Hostility grew between the white and red leaders. An awful thunderstorm in August, with vicious shafts of lightning, wrecked the Indian harvest, burned the green meadows, and killed the birds in the fields. Superstitious Saturiba believed that the storm was a French cannonade.

Quickly isolated from Indian friends, Laudonnière earned new enemies when some of his crew turned to piracy. The Spaniards reported at least one incident off Yaguana, on the west coast of Hispaniola, where hides and sugar were stolen and the Spanish crews thrown overboard before the French returned to Fort Caroline. But the hunger of Laudonnière's colony grew from day to day and their old Indian friends, knowing they were masters of the situation, demanded the shirts off French backs in exchange for a single fish. Relieved of all fear of the white men, whose fort had begun to fall apart, the Indians offered a little cornmeal or fish in the hope of luring the French into an ambush. Many calamities followed.

Vainly Laudonnière stood on Saint Johns Bluff and gazed toward the horizon, praying for the provisions promised from his homeland. Then one day a fleet appeared, but Laudonnière still watched with a tortured heart. Were they friend or foe? The vessels were under the command of Master John Hawkins—who, like his father, was a famous English slave trader—and were bound for England after having captured Negroes on the Guinea coast and sold them to the Spaniards in the West Indies "at the point of a sword." Only one of his three ships was truly impressive—the *Jesus of Lübeck,* a magnificent frigate of seven hundred tons and the personal property of Queen Elizabeth I.

Laudonnière was plunged into a dilemma. Was France still at war with England? Hawkins, a congenial fellow when not stealing Negroes and throwing them into the holds of his vessels, did not quite disarm Laudonnière, especially after he offered to carry all the French to their homeland. Laudonnière, suspecting that he might become a victim of the "scurviest" trick ever played by one nation upon another, refused the offer.

Soon he was plagued by a new mutiny of those who wished to return to France. Hawkins remained good-humored. He offered a small vessel for which Laudonnière could pay in artillery and powder (the French leader, distrusting the "cupidity" of Elizabeth I, did not mention the silver he possessed). The jovial Hawkins sold to the remaining French provisions and fifty pairs of shoes, accepting Laudonnière's "note of hand" in payment. He agreed to carry to England the goods the French pirates had stolen, and left two Englishmen as hostages at Fort Caroline to guarantee that nothing should go amiss in this transaction.

Fair winds blew in August and Hawkins sailed away.

If Laudonnière patted his stomach with satisfaction, he did not realize what deep trouble he was in on both sides of the Atlantic.

The Protestant leaders in Paris were scandalized by the reports they received of Laudonnière's behavior. No king could act more tyrannically and cruelly than he. By what authority had he taken women to Fort Caroline? To investigate the depravities of Laudonnière, a new expedition was authorized under Jean Ribaut. Seven vessels—one under the command of Ribaut's son, Jacques —sailed from Dieppe early in May. They carried about three hundred new colonists, including soldiers bearing a type of portable firearm called an arquebus, or harquebus.

Ribaut appeared at the mouth of the Saint Johns River almost at the moment in late August 1565 when the survivors at Fort Caroline prepared to depart. Laudonnière aimed two small fieldpieces at the advancing fleet. But by luck Ribaut's long beard was recognized, battle was averted, and the two Frenchmen fell into one another's arms. Laudonnière explained away all fears, including the fact that, after all, the women were only chambermaids. Ribaut decided to stay to assist in the defense of Fort Caroline.

Meanwhile, through spies and rumors, the Spanish were alerted to the invasion of Florida by the French. There were reasons, both visible and invisible, why Spain objected to this intrusion. Outwardly, Spain could say that by resisting the French she wished to rid the West Indies of piracy and to reduce Fort Caroline as a threat to the Bahama Channel, through which the Spanish treasure fleets passed.

But Spain's "inward" reasons were more compelling. In those middle years of the sixteenth century, Catholicism in Spain came so close to fanaticism that any Protestant, or "Lutheran," was a mortal enemy. A hypnotic spell seemed cast over the Spanish court and all associated with it. Phrases like "the service of God" and "the spiritual welfare" of civilization were so often repeated that human delusion grew into holy command.

In this spirit, the fleet of Don Pedro Menéndez de Avilés, admiral of Spain, believed to consist of the finest trained seamen and commanders, was dispatched to free Florida from Ribaut and Laudonnière. The superstitious Spanish were always cheered by what they called "godly omens," and so they applauded the report that 150 Frenchmen, in search of provisions, had been captured by the Indians and all but six had been eaten in a cannibalistic feast.

Menéndez's fleet was sorely damaged in its voyage from Cádiz. Common sense should have dictated that instead of seeking harbor in Florida he should winter in Havana, where he could be refitted and reinforced. But Menéndez, afraid that his crippled fleet could not reach Havana without being run down and destroyed by the French, made an opposite decision—he would destroy Ribaut's ships anchored in the entrance to the Saint Johns River. An almost comic opera developed as the Spaniards faced the French at this point. To appreciate the scene, one must remember how dramatic voices can sound in the stillness of becalmed water and an echoing forest. "Very courteously," the records say, Menéndez called first:

"Gentlemen, from where does this fleet come?"

"From France," a voice answered.

"What are you doing here?"

"Bringing infantry, artillery, and supplies for a fort which the king of France has in this country, and for others which he is going to make."

Even the birds seemed to stop chattering in the pause that followed. Then a Spanish voice called:

"Are you Catholics or Lutherans?"

"Lutherans," came the reply, "and our general is Jean Ribaut." The French then addressed the same questions to the Spaniards.

Menéndez decided to answer:

"I am the general," he said. "My name is Pedro Menéndez de Avilés. This is the armada of the king of Spain, who has sent me to burn and hang the Lutheran French who should be found here, and in the morning I will board your ships; and if I find any Catholics they will be well treated."

Ribaut outwitted his challengers by sailing his ships through the Spanish fleet. The French vessels scattered north and south and soon outran their enemy.

Thus began the war for Florida. Ribaut, recalling his fleet, followed Menéndez back to Saint Augustine Harbor, and the members of the French crew said that they drank "to the head of Pedro Menéndez and those with him. Cursed Spaniards! We will hang them from the yardarms of their own ships as well as from ours, so that they will not come again to smell out this country of ours!"

Actually nothing was decided at sea—Ribaut's ships were too fleet for the Spaniards to overtake and Menéndez's vessels too well armed for the French to capture. An attack by Ribaut on Menéndez's fleet was thwarted by the Spaniard's luck in getting part of his ships over the low sandbar in Saint Augustine Harbor. Then a "norther" —the most violent wind in the memory of living Indians —ended any hope of a coastal attack. Ribaut's fleet limped back to the protection of Fort Caroline. So sure were the Spaniards that God had favored them, they celebrated the Mass of the Holy Ghost.

In 1566 Menéndez decided that only by an overland attack could the French be vanquished. Since sacred days were considered good omens for starting any enterprise, Menéndez began his preparations on September 16, a holy day. Menéndez placed the fleet at Saint Augustine in charge of his brother Bartolomé. Drums, trumpets, fifes, and ringing bells called to muster the three hundred arquebusmen and two hundred pikesmen Menéndez was taking with him. Each carried on his back his weapons, a bottle of wine, and six pounds of biscuit. Two Indian chiefs who had been abused by the French offered to show the way, and to Menéndez they were "angels sent by God." A Frenchman with hands tied behind his back also was taken along. Twenty axmen went in advance to blaze a trail through forests and swamps.

In a pelting rain that fell almost incessantly for the next four days and nights, the Spaniards started. In one hand Menéndez held a compass and in the other the rope that bound the French captive. Forward they all sloshed, the water never lower than their knees. Soldiers unable to swim the creeks and streams they encountered were carried across on pikes. Clothes became soaked, their food spoiled, and their gunpowder was wet. Menéndez pretended not to hear the grumblers even when, in the storm darkness, the trail was missed.

The attack on Fort Caroline was launched on September 20—a good day for the superstitious Spaniards since it marked the feast of Saint Matthew. A sympathetic commander of Fort Caroline had excused his rain-soaked sentinels, accounting for the surprise with which Menéndez struck the fort. Frenchmen tumbled out of their beds and quarters—some half dressed, some naked, some in nightshirts. French blood covered the ground. Mercilessly the Spaniards bore down, slashing with knives and swords. One occupant of the fort later declared he could "find no greater cruelty among the wild beasts." A few escaped into the forest or aboard Ribaut's ships. Menéndez offered to spare the women and children if the French promised to take them home at once. When he was refused, angered Spaniards used daggers to rip out the eyeballs of the dead and hurl them with loud curses at the French ships.

Within an hour the victory was achieved. Of 240 French within the fort, 132 were already dead. No Spaniard was killed and only one was wounded. Among the captives were fifty women and children and "half a dozen drummers and trumpeters." Six boxes of books considered heretical by the Spanish were burned. Into the same blaze went packs of playing cards, for on their backs were pictures that mocked saints and other holy objects. Whenever Menéndez ordered a prisoner hanged, he announced solemnly: "I do this not to Frenchmen, but to Lutherans."

When Menéndez returned to Saint Augustine, he learned from the Indians that Ribaut's fleet had been shipwrecked in a storm. The starving survivors were easily rounded up and slaughtered.

In time, Spain would send more humane colonizers in Jesuit priests. Yet these religious gentlemen were no less ambitious than Menéndez, and by 1571 their missions among the Indians had reached to the Potomac River—not far from present-day Washington, D.C.

Chapter 4

AN AGGRESSIVE QUEEN
England Rediscovers the New World

Spain would soon discover that her claims to the Atlantic seacoast of the New World were to be challenged by foes far more formidable than the French. After all, the English, through the voyages of the Cabots, could make claims going back to the time of Columbus. True, Henry VII, the first of the Tudors, had quickly lost interest in explorations; but Elizabeth I, the last of the Tudors, possessed a different nature. She was deeply angered at the arrogance of the wealthy Spanish in planting spies in every European court. Now, before Spain grew any stronger, was the moment to put these old enemies in their place, Elizabeth decided. In this spirit the queen could pretend not to hear stories of the depravations of British pirates like Hawkins, as long as they preyed on the Spanish or the French. Martin Frobisher made three voyages to Labrador in the 1570s in a vain search for gold and a northwest passage to the Indies. Then in 1577 Francis Drake set off in the *Golden Hind* on a three-year voyage around the world, proof that England had decided to become a major seapower. Drake, as Spain discovered to her sorrow, was outstanding among a new breed of "explorer-pirates." Drake not only plundered treasures, mostly from the Spanish, worth millions of dollars—which the queen happily tucked away in the Tower of London—but explored the Pacific coast as far north as British Columbia.

Not every venture proved successful for the queen, who had determined to be rid of Spanish domination. Sir Humphrey Gilbert (a half brother of Sir Walter Raleigh) was sent on two secretive voyages of a somewhat questionable purpose. Gilbert sought both a northeast and a northwest passage to the Indies. The first voyage, in 1578, charged him "to search, find out and view such remote, heathen and barbarous lands, countries and territories not actually possessed of any Christian people or prince." Apparently he found none. His second voyage, in 1583, was especially important because in Newfoundland he established a claim for the first English colony in North America. On the voyage home the nobleman's bark, *Squirrel,* sank and Sir Gilbert drowned.

The faith of Elizabeth I in future naval accomplishments remained unshaken. The fact that Spanish vessels patrolled the coast of Florida and the Carolinas and that the Spaniards included the future state of Virginia as part of their North American domain did not trouble the queen. She would go her own way and let the Spaniards be hanged!

So, on a bright April day in 1584, two British barks commanded by Capt. Philip Amadas and Capt. Arthur Barlowe left England in search of a site for a future colony along the southern part of the North American coast. The low-lying coast of future North Carolina beckoned to these explorers, and an island later called Roanoke especially attracted them.

Such rapturous reports of a new land rarely had come to the ears of Elizabeth I as those returned by Amadas and Barlowe. The Indians of the coast here, she heard, were the "most gentle, loving and faithful, void of all guile and treason." A fleet, commanded by Sir Richard Grenville, carried the first colonists to Roanoke Island in June of 1585. Grenville announced the place as belonging to "her Majesty's new kingdom of Virginia" and described the mainland as "the goodliest soil under heaven." To Grenville "sweet trees" and grapes excelled any found in France, Spain, or Italy. He discovered "many sorts of apothecary drugs"—and, contradictorily, not a native who gave evidence of a day's illness. Grenville doubted if a better spot for a colony existed in all Christendom.

Grenville left about a hundred colonists on Roanoke and sailed home for new supplies. The settlers were not overly intelligent. They failed to cultivate the land, wasted time searching for gold, and picked quarrels with the Indians. Soon they were desperately longing to be back in England. They could not know, of course, that for weeks Drake, who was now Sir Francis, had been raiding Spanish ships and towns in the West Indies and had pillaged and burned Saint Augustine. Terror-stricken Spaniards came from their hiding places in the surrounding swamps as Drake sailed on to Roanoke. While he was there a terrific storm—possibly a hurricane —burst upon the discouraged colonists, further crushing their spirits as they were forced to cling to trees for their lives. Drake had intended merely to take back some of the sick and unfit, but now pity touched him at the sight of the hurricane survivors, who seemed as bent in spirit as the trees. He carried the settlers home to England.

Now the promised supply ship arrived to find the colonists gone, so it turned back. Almost in its wake Grenville reached Roanoke with three ships. For days he coasted north and south, trying in vain to discover what had happened to his colony. Sir Richard was not one to surrender title to the country. But the fifteen men he left behind with two years' provisions to hold the fort on Roanoke must have made a forlorn picture as Grenville sailed away.

The next year still another expedition, under John White, brought a fresh load of colonists to Roanoke. He found only wilderness. Where was the fort? Where was there so much as a single skeleton of the fifteen men left by Grenville? White rebuilt the fort and a few houses, giving to the new settlement the name of "the Citie of Raleigh in Virginia." In August White chestily bragged over his granddaughter, Virginia Dare, the first child of English parents born in North America. He sailed home to England, promising that he would return with dispatch.

A man more honest than John White could not have been found. But the histories of men and nations move in unexpected, mysterious cycles. England was bitterly at war with Spain, facing its great armada of 130 vessels, 2,500 guns, and 30,000 men. Storms which wrecked the Spanish fleet helped the plucky English, who said with a touch of reverence behind their laughter, "God blew and they were scattered."

Four years passed while John White cursed every calm that delayed his return to Roanoke. At last, in 1590, he landed on a deserted island. No person, no stick of furniture remained. Books were torn from their covers. Here and there he found a piece of armor "almost eaten through with rust." On one tree he found the word CROATOAN. On another only the first three letters, CRO, appeared.

Why? What had happened?

Had Spaniards murdered the English colonists?

Had they been slaughtered by the Indians—or, equally plausible, had they simply wandered off to dwell with the red men?

The mystery of the "Lost Colony of Roanoke" never has been solved. In 1603 Queen Elizabeth died, not knowing how close England was to planting her first permanent colony in America—and with it her language and many of her political and cultural traditions.

Chapter 5

JAMESTOWN
The English Succeed

A chilly London fog, rising from the Thames, hung over a Blackwall dock in late December of 1606. Waiting Englishmen, drawing shawls around their shoulders, wished that they were home and already gnawing their mutton chops. Queen Elizabeth I now was dead and James I, the thrifty Scot who had succeeded her to the throne three years ago, liked old shoes, old ideas, old habits. James I came to the throne when England was changing from feudalism to capitalism. He entered a London where beggars filled the streets, while vagabonds boldly stole from travelers on country roads. Prices soared, wages sank to new levels of starvation. People went to bed hungry. They awoke in the morning without work or hope.

Playwrights saw only one escape from this misery—the New World—and so in 1605 the hero of a popular English drama, *Eastward, Ho!* spoke these optimistic lines:

> I tell thee golde is more plentifull in Virginia than copper is with us, and for as much redde copper as I can bring, I will have thrice the weight in gould. All their dripping pans and chamber potts are pure gould, and all the chaines with which they chaine up the streets are massie gould; all the prisoners they take goe fettered in gould, and for rubies and diamonds, they goe forth in holidays and gather them by the seashore to hang on their children's coates and sticke in their children's caps as commonally as our children wear saffron, gilt brooches and groates [silver coins] with hoales in them.

Eastward, Ho! certainly accounted in part for the shawled figures who gathered at the Blackwall dock to watch their relatives and friends board the three ships that the newly organized Virginia Company of London had equipped by royal charter to send to North America for tentative explorations south of latitude 38—the *Susan Constant,* one hundred tons; the *Godspeed,* forty tons; and the *Discovery,* a pinnace of twenty tons. No one spoke of the lost colony of Roanoke, for had it not been ships like these that had earned bountiful profits on voyages to Muscovy, the Levant, Guinea, and India?

Why should not the New World pay off as well?

In command of the little fleet was an experienced mariner, Capt. Christopher Newport, who felt at ease with his passengers of noble and lowly status. Capt. Bartholomew Gosnold (who, two years earlier, had explored the islands and bays off Cape Cod) commanded the *Godspeed*. Among the voyagers was Master George Percy, eighth son of Henry, eighth earl of Northumberland, whose *Observations* on this voyage reads like a tale out of the *Arabian Nights*.

On December 20, 1606, moorings were cast loose from the Blackwall dock. Following the Thames, the fleet reached the Kentish shore by January 5. Winds and storms raked the ocean, but here the boats were protected by the Goodwin Sands. At last the gale subsided and the Englishmen proceeded toward Virginia. Long, hard weeks followed, exhausting both their bodies and their supplies. Then, on February 12, Percy observed a blazing star in the sky. It was the first incident Percy recorded, as though this sight refreshed his hope that they were not forever lost.

On March 23 the fleet reached the West Indies, just as the sun was burning off the morning mists. The crews of the boats sailed through a strange world, watching a whale fighting a thresher shark and a swordfish, taking hot baths for their health on the French possession of

Marie Galante, and encamping six days on the island of
Saint Nevis to throw off the illnesses the long voyage
may have produced. Fear-stricken Indians disappeared
among the mountaintops, a relief to everyone. The voyagers killed wild boars and iguanas with speckled bellies
on Puerto Rico, but grieved when "one Edward Brookes
Gentleman" died because his "fat melted within him."

Storms, an old story now, brought delays, but on
April 26, "without any let or hindrance," the ships
reached the entrance to Chesapeake Bay. A small party,
going ashore, was attacked by Indians "creeping upon
all foure, from the Hills, like Beares, with their Bowes in
their mouthes." A captain was "hurt" on both hands, a
sailor was twice wounded. Night came on. Hostilities
ceased. By daylight the English ships passed between
the capes that one day would be called Charles and
Henry.

Thus they entered the fairyland of Chesapeake Bay.
From day to day, great rivers awaited discovery, but
Percy caught the true romance for hungry sailors. Here
mussels and oysters "lay on the ground as thicke as
stones"; here strawberries were "foure times bigger and
better than ours in England." On Hampton Creek, Percy
recorded, Indians "goe altogether naked, but their
privities are covered." In a dance of welcome "one of the
Savages" stood in the middle of the group, singing as he
beat one hand against the other. Fellow Indians danced
around him—some shouting and howling, some stamping
against the ground, some with "many anticke tricks and
faces, making noise like so many Wolves or Devils."

Percy possessed marvelous descriptive powers. Entering the James, he observed a sachem "playing on a Flute made of a Reed, with a Crown of Deares haire colloured red, in fashion of a Rose fastened about his knot of haire, and a great Plate of Copper on the other side of his head, with two long Feathers in fashion of a paire of Hornes placed in the midst of his Crowne." The sachem's body was painted crimson, his face stained blue. Bracelets of pearls were suspended from earlobes in which were set bird claws decorated with copper and gold.

On May 8, attempting to enter the Indian lands drained by the Appomattox River, the Englishmen were suddenly appalled. Indians opposed them, armed with weapons "able to cleave a man in sunder"; the chief stood before them "cross-legged," demanding that they "be gone." They went.

Four days later they found an inlet about five miles from present-day Williamsburg—they called it "Archer's Hope"—where the soil looked "good and fruitfull," the timber was excellent, and vines as big as a man's thigh wound their way to the treetops. Squirrels raced across the ground and up the trees. Turkeys nested everywhere; it was difficult not to step on their eggs. Wings of dark red, crimson, and pale blue filled the air as birds flew overhead. But the ships could not ride "neere the shore." Next day, May 13, a "seating place" was selected for a reason that Percy described: "Our shippes doe lie so neere the shoare that they are moored to the Trees in six fathom water."

In honor of the thrifty Scot who then occupied the throne of England, the settlement was called variously James Fort, James Towne, and James Citty.

Outwardly, Jamestown seemed idyllic. Woods of birch, oak, cedar, cypress, walnut, and sassafras grew in abundance. Upon every hillside, like blankets of wild color, were spread strawberries, mulberries, raspberries, and other fruits. The James and its connecting streams teemed with fish. In lush meadows could be found deer, bears, foxes, otters, beavers, muskrats, "and wild beasts unknown."

With good sense, the colonists began at once to build a fort. Indians, appearing that first night, fled in terror, but daylight brought two more red men, announcing that their sachem was coming and all "would be merry" with a "fat Deare." The chief arrived next day, accompanied by a hundred armed men. He wanted the settlers to lay their arms aside, which, wisely, they did not. An Indian, detected stealing a hatchet, was shot. A second Indian dashed at the white man with a wooden sword, "thinking to beat out his braines," and failed. Two days later the Indians sent over a deer, with forty men to carry it, but, as Percy guessed, they came "more in villanie than any love they bare us." Again, the trick did not work.

Percy saw strange sights along the James. One was a boy, about ten years old, with "a head of haire of a perfect yellow and a reasonable white skinne." Could the lad be a descendant of one of the settlers of the lost colony of Roanoke? Again, another miracle to Percy, he observed an Indian "above eight score yeeres of age." The Indian's eyes were sunken, his hair was gray, and his beard white (Indians were not supposed to have facial hair). His gummy mouth was toothless, but, as Percy conceded with an ill-disguised envy, "This Savage was as lusty and went as fast as any of us."

Capt. John Smith was the spectacular character at Jamestown. If he was a liar, he was a good one. By his own account, Smith was born in Lincolnshire, England, in January of 1579, the first son of tenants on the estate of Lord Willoughby. He was apprenticed to a tradesman at the age of fifteen, and ran away.

His *Autobiography* is a rare romance. He fought in the Netherlands, among other countries; he captured a thief; was thrown overboard from a ship and stranded on an isolated island and rescued; next he engaged in a desperate sea fight, which taught him how to plan and win battles. He fought Turks in Transylvania, a province of Romania, and, left for dead, was revived and taken to Constantinople as a slave. Here he won the love of the wife of the Turkish pasha, who by various means arranged for his escape (including knocking out a fellow's brains and running off with the dead man's clothes). Flight across the desert brought him to a Russian garrison; thereafter his travels across Europe brought him to England just in time to sign on one of the Virginia Company's ships as a prospective planter in Virginia.

Others "envying his repute" was the only reason John Smith gave for his enemies. He knew by the time that the Jamestown voyagers reached Dominica in the West

Indies he was the victim of "scandalous suggestions" that he intended to murder the members of the council and make himself king. He was taken prisoner as a result of these false charges. On April 26, when the ships entered Chesapeake Bay, a box given in London containing instructions for the management of the colony was unsealed. Smith was among the seven appointed to a council empowered to elect its own president, but as he was under arrest he was not allowed to participate in the government of the settlement. The choice of Edward Maria Wingfield as president of the council left deep roots of resentment within Capt. John Smith, especially when Wingfield listed him simply as a planter and not as a member of the council.

Smith nursed his grudge. "The Precidents overweening jealousie," he wrote, "would admit no exercise at armes, or fortification but the boughs of trees cast together in the forme of a halfe moone by the extraordinary paines and diligence of Captaine Kendall."

Meanwhile captains Newport and Smith sailed up the river, passed the pleasant hillside village of Powhatan, and discovered the Falls of the James. Specks of yellow glittering in the water so fascinated Newport that he loaded his vessel with worthless pieces of mica. His return to Jamestown was a shock. As Smith had expected, Wingfield had wrought chaos within the settlement. The Indians attacked, "17 men [were] hurt and a boy slaine," and had not a shot from a crossbow felled the bough of a tree among the savages, causing confusion, all the colonists might have been killed.

At last, Smith wrote snippishly, Wingfield "was contented" to construct a sensible fort. A triangular bastion faced river, woods, and swamp, and at each corner a bulwark, shaped like a half moon, mounted powerful demiculverins, or small cannons. A church, storehouse, and flimsily built houses rose within the fort. Smith, no longer considered a "prisoner," was admitted to the council.

But it was humid summer now. Food spoiled, drinking water became infected, and by the end of September illness was so commonplace that the original 140 settlers had dwindled to 50. A few, to be sure, had crowded aboard the ship when Newport sailed home with his cargo of useless mica.

Cheerier times were ahead, especially after 1608 when Smith became the colony's chief councilor. When Captain Newport returned with a Second Supply of settlers that year, Jamestown's population increased to 110, and Ann Barras, maidservant, married John Laydon, carpenter, in the first recorded English wedding in North America. A Third Supply in 1609 numbered approximately four hundred, but about one third of this group represented the scrapings of the London streets. They were lazy, slipshod, and dissipated, and many succumbed from the fevers and plagues that thrived in the swamps. The winter of 1609–10 became the dreadful "starving time." Smith, who had returned to England, gave a hearsay account of the anguish of those poor devils who remained:

> ...as for corne provision and contribution from the Salvages, we had nothing but mortall wounds, with clubs

and arrowes; as for our Hogs, Hens, Goats, Sheepe, Horse,
or what lived, our commanders, officers and Salvages
daily consumed them, some small proportions sometimes
we tasted, till all was devoured; . . . of five hundred . . .
there remained not past sixtie men, women and children,
most miserable and poore creatures; and those were
preserved for the most part, by roots, herbes, acornes,
walnuts, berries, now and then a little fish; they that had
startch in these extremities, made no small use of it; yea,
even the very skinnes of our horses. Nay, so great was
our famine, that a Salvage we slew and buried, the
poorer sort tooke him up againe and eat him; and so did
divers one another boyled and stewed with roots and
herbs: And one amongst the rest did kill his wife, powdered [salted] her, and had eaten part of her before it
was knowne; for which hee was executed, as hee well
deserved: now whether shee was better roasted, boyled
or carbonado'd [broiled], I know not; but of such a dish
as powdered wife I never heard of. . . .

The leaderless colony sank into indolence and vice,
and when two vessels under Sir Thomas Gates came up
the James in May of 1610, he offered to carry the survivors to Newfoundland, his true destination. Everyone
was willing to go. By one of the strangest coincidences
in history, a storm delayed their departure by a day, or
otherwise they would not have met Lord Delaware
arriving with new supplies. Delaware talked the settlers
into returning to Jamestown.

In London the subscribers to the Virginia colony
were discouraged over the lack of profits from year to

year. Gates, back in England, revived their hopes, and even though some financial supporters withdrew, Gates won enough assistance so that in August of 1611 he returned to Jamestown in six vessels with three hundred men, one hundred head of cattle, and various other provisions. Naming himself governor, Gates intended making religion the foundation of law and order.

But the true salvation of Jamestown came from an unexpected source.

John Rolfe had sailed with Gates's fleet in 1610, but, driven off course by the wind, became shipwrecked in the Bermudas (an incident believed to have inspired Shakespeare's *The Tempest*). Both Rolfe's wife and baby daughter, named Bermuda, died before Rolfe, a hard-headed man, could build a ship and continue his voyage to Jamestown. With him he brought the seeds of the tobacco grown in the Caribbean.

Whether or not Pocahontas saved the life of Capt. John Smith may be accepted as history or legend. Jamestown first saw Powhatan's daughter as a naked child who amused the settlers with her lively dancing and spinning cartwheels. Then John Rolfe arrived. He fell in love with Pocahontas. In a letter to Sir Thomas Dale, now governor of the Jamestown colony, Rolfe revealed a self-torment rare in English literature:

What should I doe? shall I be of so untoward a disposition as to refuse to leade the blinde into the right way? Shall I be so unnaturall, as not to give bread to the

hungrie? or uncharitable, as not to cover the naked?
Shall I despise to actuate the pious dueties of a Christian? Shall the base feare of displeasing the world, over-
power and with holde mee from revealing unto man these
spirituall workes of the Lord, which in my meditations
and praiers, I have daily made knowne unto him? God
forbid.

In "clearness of my conscience" and "clean from the
filth and impurity," Rolfe married Pocahontas, in the
village chapel at Jamestown, in 1614. Pocahontas wore
a tunic of white muslin, over which hung a handsome
robe that she had embroidered. A band of glittering
feathers covered her hair. A white bridal veil hung over
her face. Rolfe took his bride to England, where she was
known as Lady Rebecca, her Christian name. The London countryside soon abounded with taverns called "La
Belle Sauvage."

Stricken with smallpox, Lady Rebecca, or Pocahontas,
died in England. Rolfe left their son, Thomas, to be
educated in the British Isles, while in May of 1617 he
made the lonely journey back to Jamestown. Ultimately
Thomas would migrate to Virginia, where he would become a prosperous planter. By then the type of tobacco
the elder Rolfe had brought from the Caribbean grew
so well in Virginia soil, and proved so profitable, that it
was even grown in the streets between the houses!

There was an ironic humor in this situation, for James
I was so opposed to the "filthie noveltie" of smoking that
he wrote a pamphlet, *A Counterblaste to Tobacco*, in
which he expressed his anger toward this "custome loth-

some to the eye, hatefull to the Nose, harmefull to the braine, dangerous to the Lung, and in the blacke stinking fume thereof, neerest resembling the horrible Stigian smoke of the pit that is bottomless." James I claimed that when the corpse of a smoker was opened, a bushel of soot was found within!

But suddenly James I maintained a discreet silence on the subject. The king knew when he had his hand on a good thing. Glassmaking, silkworms, timber, soap ashes, and the medicinal uses of sassafras all had failed to make the Virginia adventure profitable; now tobacco had tipped the scale the other way. James I never gave up anything without claiming his shilling's worth—including a prejudice, in all probability—but his lips now were sealed.

Spain eyed warily the growth of the English settlements at Jamestown and elsewhere along the river. A Spanish caravel anchored off Point Comfort in 1611, looking for a pilot. The three Spaniards who went ashore were captured by the English, and five years elapsed before Governor Dale consented to return them to Europe. One died at sea and another, Francisco Lembri, proved to be an English subject and was hanged as a traitor. Not until 1618 was the surviving spy, Don Diego de Molina, able to return to Spain. He rushed to the king with a glowing account of Virginia and its reputed silver mine. Moreover, Molina declared, if Spain wished to "stop the progress of a hydra in its infancy," now was the time to act. Molina did not lack for fervor in describing how easily he could conquer Virginia:

... With eight hundred or one thousand soldiers he [the king] could reduce this place with great ease, or even with five hundred, because there is no expectation of aid from England for resistance and the forts which they have are of boards and so weak that a kick would break them down, and once arrive at the ramparts those without would have the advantage over those within because its beams and loopholes are common to both parts—a fortification without skill and made by unskilled men. ...

The king responded apathetically, giving him men, Molina wrote disgustedly, who were "poorly drilled and not prepared for military action." The truth was that at that moment Spain was not anxious for any further entanglement with the British.

Chapter 6

SEEDS OF LIBERTY
Self-Government Comes to Jamestown

A sad event occurred in Jamestown in 1619. That November a Dutch ship appeared with a cargo of twenty-odd Negro slaves. Badly in need of provisions and having neither money nor other merchandise to offer, the Dutch captain proposed exchanging the slaves for his requirements. Reluctantly the Virginians agreed; they had no real use for slaves.

But that same year a triumph had been achieved

when under Governor Sir George Yeardley the first legislative assembly in America convened in the choir of the Jamestown church on July 30. In addition to the members of the council, two delegates each were sent from the settlements of James "citty," Charles "citty," Henrico, Kiccowtan (later Elizabeth City), and from seven plantations situated on the north and south banks of the James. "Forasmuche as men's affaires doe little prosper where God's service is neglected," the assembly opened with a prayer and the taking of the oath of allegiance to the king. Two delegates from the plantations who had not been members of the Virginia colony long enough were sent home in the conviction that they could not bring "fair representation" to the problems that must be considered by this House of Burgesses, as the assembly was called. A Captain Martin was severely reprimanded for forcing the Indians to trade with him. "Suche outrages as this," read the minutes, "might breede danger and loss of life to others of the Colony."

Clearly America's first legislative body understood the fundamental purpose of self-government. Still, Sir George Yeardley, only recently knighted by James I, brought a warning "not to correcte or controll anything" on their own initiative, but only if they judged "any lawe . . . did presse or binde too harde, that we might by waye of humble petition, seeke to have it redressed, especially because this great Charter is to bind us and our heyers for ever."

Six petitions reached Sir George the following day. A complete clarification of past land grants was requested. Another asked to "allowe to the male children, of them and all others begotten in Virginia, being the onely hope of a posterity, a single share a piece, and shares for their issue or for themselves, because that in a newe plantation it is not knowen whether man or woman be more necessary." A third petition urged the appointment of a subtreasurer to collect land rents; a fourth urged that "workmen of all sortes, fitt for that purpose" be sent from England to build a "University and College"; another asked "to change the savage name of Kiccowtan." The burgesses knew what held their skin and bones together; they set prices for tobacco at three shillings a pound for the best quality grown and eighteen pence a pound for tobacco of "the second sorte."

The lawmakers observed the Sabbath, but were hard back at their labors next day. Human nature, they realized, could change in a wilderness—not always for the better—and so, in a very real sense, their laws reflected an effort to protect the settler from himself. They listened to Rolfe's description of "wicked instigations, hatched by him who seeketh and delighteth in mans destruction," and so they decreed "that no injury or oppression be wrought by the English against the Indian whereby the present peace might be disturbed and antient quarrells might be revived."

They dealt harshly with their own shortcomings. Idleness they held "in detestation" and an "Idler," though a freedman, was punished by being put to work until "he shewe apparent signes of amendment." Gambling at cards and dice was discouraged by forcing the winners to forfeit all their gains. Winners and losers alike were each to forfeit ten shillings, one tenth of this amount "to go to the discoverer" and the remainder "to charitable and pious uses in the Incorporation where the faulte is comitted."

Drunkenness carried a series of punishments. For a first offense the culprit was "to be reprooved privately by the Minister" and for a second he was to be lectured "publiquely." Thereafter the drunkard was "to lye in boltes [iron leg bands] 12 howers in the house of the Provost Marshall and to paye his fee." Officers of the colony who were found drunk were dealt with even more severely. Other laws provided reprimands "against excesse in apparell."

Relations with Indians were strictly regulated. Whenever in deer hunting, fishing, beating of corn, or other work intercourse with Indians was necessary, the governor's consent had to be obtained for more than five or six Indians to participate in these enterprises since, the governor said, the Indians "are a most treacherous people and quickly gone when they have done a villany." Indians must be lodged "apart." Looking toward the future, the burgesses decided "that for laying a surer foundation of the conversion of the Indians to Christian Religion, eache towne, citty, Borrough, and particular plantation do obtaine unto themselves by just means a certaine number of the natives' children to be educated by them in true religion and civile course of life—of which children the most towardly boyes in witt and graces of nature to be brought up by them in the first elements of literature, so to be fitted for the Colledge intended for them that from thence they may be sente to that worke of conversion."

A set of laws was necessary for the systematic cultivation of corn, mulberry trees, silk-flax, aniseed, and vineyards. Tobacco, still the colony's bulwark, must be carefully cured or "it shall there immediately be burnt before the owner's face."

The dog days of August had now overtaken the burgesses. The session ended with "a third sorte of lawes (suche as might proceed out of every man's private conceipt)." No English "dog of quality" or any arms could be sold or exchanged with an Indian. Without the governor's permission, a settler could not visit an Indian town, nor could he be absent from his lodgings for more than seven days without similar consent. Excommunication from church and seizure of personal property could punish "enormous sinnes." Swearing, after three offenses, cost a freedman five shillings, a servant a public whipping. Equally severe was the law which regulated marriage:

> No maide or woman servant, either now resident in the Colonie or hereafter to come, shall contract herselfe in marriage without either the consente of her parents, or of her Mr or Mris, or of the magistrate and minister of the place both together. And whatsoever minister shall marry or contracte any suche persons without some of the foresaid consentes shalbe subjecte to the severe censure of the Governor and Counsell of Estate.

The work of the House of Burgesses of Virginia would continue for 157 years.

Before returning to England in 1609, Capt. John Smith's adventuresome spirit led him to explore every cove or river that emptied into Chesapeake Bay, and at last he discovered the island at the mouth of the Susquehanna River. The story of this find Smith carried back to an old friend at Jamestown, Edward Palmer, who happened by royal charter to own this land. A graduate of Oxford's Magdalene College in 1572, Palmer visited these "two miles whereof the Southwest is very good land and at the Northwest end is very high rocke."

Palmer, a man of "plenteous means," inspected the island. He had no interest whatever in making a profit from trading beaver pelts. He was described, quite accurately, as a "diligent antiquarian," intensely interested in old coins and pottery. Books found on Palmer's Isle proved that he actually lived there for a time. A dream entranced him. Why should not the campus of the first university in North America, modeled after Oxford, rise on this island? Palmer spent thousands of pounds planning a university with such modern curricula as courses in painting in oils and water colors. Unfortunately, Palmer died before his plans could be realized, and with him died the first hope for an Oxford in America.

To win the approval of Chief Opechancanough, who succeeded Powhatan, the English built a house for him with a lock and key. So amused was the chief by the latter gift that some believed he opened and locked his door at least a hundred times a day. His braves roamed like friends through the fields of the settlers, but an Indian known as Jack of the Feather boasted he was "immortall from any hurt [that] could bee done him by the English." Early in March of 1622, Jack persuaded a planter named Morgan to accompany him on a trading trip. The planter was murdered, and Jack appeared two or three days later wearing the white man's cap. John Smith, in his *Generall Historie of Virginia*, stated succinctly how the colonists reacted:

"Jack so moved their patience, they shot him."

Opechancanough, who adored Jack, was crushed with grief. No longer would he play with his key and lock. Although he instructed his warriors to maintain a cheerful outer countenance, Opechancanough planned a dreadful revenge. Living in groups of thirty, forty, and fifty, the Indians appeared to offer no concentrated threat, even to plantation dwellers whose lands now reached as far as fifty or sixty miles up both sides of the river from Jamestown. Indeed, many Indians brought gifts and breakfasted with these colonists on Good Friday, 1622, before the red men fell to the deviltry.

Smith, who spent his last years writing many books about New England and Virginia, described how, seizing any tools or weapons they found about the houses, the Indians "slew most barbarously, not sparing age or sex, man, woman or childe." The slaughter, Smith added, was so quickly executed "that few or none discerned the weapon or blow that brought them to destruction." Workers in the field, approached by smiling Indians, suffered as cruelly. Six members of the council were killed. Captain Smith was shocked by the violence of the Indians as they "fell againe upon the dead bodies, making as well as they could a fresh murder, defacing, dragging, and mangling their dead carkases into many peeces, and carrying some parts away in derision, with base and brutish triumph."

Smith omitted few of the gory details: how the family of Capt. Nathaniel Powell was "butcher-like hagled"; how heads were chopped off; how they burned "Tobaccohouses"; how Capt. Ralph Hamor beat off the Indians "onely with spades, axes, and brickbats." The toll of the Good Friday Massacre Smith estimated at four hundred. An Indian, Chanco, who had been kindly used by the Pace family, carried the news of the fearful bloodletting to Jamestown. An alarm was spread to surrounding plantations.

Bitterness toward the Indians was deep. Luckily, wiser minds, while admitting the Indians would be easier curbed by "conquest than faire means," decided that it was their Christian duty to civilize the heathen and treat him as a friend.

Jamestown continued to prosper. In George Sandys, who had studied at but not graduated from Oxford, the colony could claim North America's first (white) poet of such eminence that his translations of Ovid and Virgil were hailed for their beauty even in England. Sandys was a real colonizer, however, a hard worker who had not come to Virginia to dream away his life. He built America's first water mill, sponsored the manufacture of iron, engaged in glassmaking (though he said the workmen sent him were "a more damned crew hell never vomited"). He revived silk and grape culture, and was called the first commercial shipbuilder in the colonies. He served Virginia as treasurer and was three times appointed to the council. Meanwhile he managed a plantation of fifteen hundred acres.

Two years after the Good Friday Massacre, Jamestown counted 124 residents and 22 houses and 3 stores. Its church was its pride. Its cattle, swine, and goats were plentiful, although there was only one horse. Its stock of arms and ammunition was sufficient. The compiling of these figures may have resulted from the wish of James I, accomplished in 1624, to dissolve the Virginia Company of London and make Virginia a royal colony.

Actually, this change little altered the course of life in Jamestown until 1635, when Sir John Harvey, the royal governor, became oppressive and tyrannical in an effort to break the independent spirit of the settlers. He struck a man who had displeased him, and committed other acts of truculence and arrogance which made him thoroughly disliked. The council considered his misdemeanors a justification for the governor's arrest and they shipped him home that same year. The king reacted very huffily to this action and ordered Harvey back to Virginia. Undaunted in spirit, the council brought the governor to trial, thus making "due process of law" one of the first fruits to blossom from the seeds of liberty planted in Jamestown. This time Harvey returned to England to stay, and Jamestown had won a victory over the Privy Council.

Chapter 7

THE MAYFLOWER COMPACT
Democracy Enters the New World

Other conflicts were developing between the crown and the colonists. One of the most important began during the reign of James I, a very stubborn old monarch who insisted that his wishes *were* the law. He had no sympathy for a group of Separatists who in religion stood for freedom of choice in the selection of preachers, in the organization of their congregations, and the conduct of their services. James I could not hide his detestation of these fanatics; how religion was practiced in England was a matter for the king and his bishops to decide. Reluctantly the Separatists realized that they must leave their homeland.

In 1607–1608 they migrated to Holland—pilgrims in a strange land—and settled in Leiden. Here out of sheer stubbornness they existed for ten years—people trained to be farmers, who were badly fitted for city life. Moreover, they were worried about their children, who tended to copy the easygoing ways of the Dutch. A whisper grew in strength. Why not try to gain refuge in the New World? By 1617 the Separatists were willing to try the new experiment and three years later they returned to England, where they were to begin their long voyage overseas.

"A very mixed lot" assembled for the voyage, including adventurers more interested in seeking treasure than religious freedom, for the Separatists by themselves did not justify the investment of a sponsoring company. Three boats were planned for the original voyage, but two leaked so badly that only the *Mayflower* was capable of attempting the journey. One hundred people, plus or minus a few, jammed the decks of this ship when on September 16, 1620, it set sail for America.

The legal destination of the *Mayflower* was Virginia, and at first fair winds carried the ship on a true course. But weather on the Atlantic can change quickly, unpredictably. Suddenly the *Mayflower* was rolling among huge waves. Destructive winds tore the sails into shreds. Leaks appeared everywhere. A main beam cracked and

sagged. A lack of lemons (a source of Vitamin C) afflicted many of the crew with scurvy, although only one
passenger died as a result of this illness.

For three reasons the Pilgrims decided that God protected them, and their successful voyage to America
constituted a sign of divine guidance:

1. The fact that only one had died of scurvy seemed
a miracle.

2. The fact that a "proud and very profane" young
sailor, cursing the Pilgrims in their misery and declaring
at least once a day how he hoped to throw half of them
overboard, himself became ill and died "in great agony"
—surely a sign that the Lord watched over them.

3. The fact that when faithful young John Howland
was swept overboard by a mighty wave, he grabbed a
line and hung on until he could be rescued with a boat-
hook.

Sixty-five treacherous days followed the embarkation
of the *Mayflower* before its passengers beheld land—not
the coast of Virginia, as was intended, but the distant
shore of Cape Cod. For half a day they tried to sail southward, but were driven back by shoals and roaring
breakers. They were not in Virginia, but in New England, where they lacked legal permission to plant a
colony.

Since some of the passengers aboard the *Mayflower*
were more interested in fortune than religious freedom,
grumblings of mutiny sounded. There was talk among
the non-Pilgrims of striking out for Virginia on foot. But
sounder minds prevailed, arguing that to survive and

settle this new country, all must remain together and draw up an agreement of laws that would protect their future. To this end, the leaders drew up the Mayflower Compact.

Forty-one "freemen" gathered in the main cabin of the *Mayflower*. Overhead a flickering fish-oil lamp showered the place with smoke whenever the door opened. Still they strained to read this document which pledged all "to enact, constitute, and frame such just and equal laws, ordinances, acts, constitutions, and offices, from time to time, as shall be thought most meet [fit] and convenient for the general good of the colony." The men made a strange assortment, ranging from stout, short-tempered Miles Standish to gentle, blue-eyed John Alden, a pair who would gain immortality in American literature through *The Courtship of Miles Standish,* a poem by Henry Wadsworth Longfellow. Each placed his signature to the compact, agreeing to live equally under the law. The date was November 21, 1620.

For weeks the *Mayflower* explored New England's sandy coast in search of a suitable harbor, so essential to establishing a successful settlement. They came at last on December 22 to a place they called Plymouth after the city in England from which they had embarked. Their first common house was completed on Christmas Day, but in only a few weeks its thatched roof was destroyed by fire.

A terrible winter followed for the Pilgrims who, expecting to settle in Virginia, had brought not a horse or cattle or a plow. Even their hooks were too large for the fish that abounded thereabouts. Sometimes two or three starving colonists perished in a single day from the rampant outbreaks of scurvy, influenza, and pneumonia. Only half the colony survived, of whom not more than six or seven enjoyed really good health.

The Indian chief who claimed the land where the Pilgrims had settled was Massasoit, who arrived one spring morning with sixty warriors and could have wiped out the colony as easily as one can pinch out the flame of a candle. Instead, he came to offer help and friendship. In the party was Squanto, who once had been captured and sold in Spain as a slave. Luck helped him to escape to the British Isles, where he became extremely proficient in speaking the English language. He conversed on easy terms with the Pilgrims, who believed that he must be a messenger from heaven.

Squanto taught the Pilgrims how to plant and cultivate corn. He taught them how to build fish traps and to stalk game. Squanto also taught them how to catch and to skin beavers, thus providing the colonists with a source of trade.

William Bradford, governor of Plymouth Colony in 1621 (he would be reelected thirty times), decreed that even the Indians should be invited to the festival of the fall harvest. New England's first Thanksgiving lasted three days. On the Sabbath the sober and gray clothes of the Pilgrims were put aside for garments of bright green and brown. They played games with the Indians. Their bellies swelled with a feast of venison, roast duck, shellfish, corn, wild berries, and fruits. Wines made from wild grapes quenched their thirst.

Unhappily, the story of Plymouth Colony did not continue in this gay pattern. A little ship, the *Fortune*, arrived in November with thirty-five settlers but few supplies. A hard winter and a summer of poor crops followed. The Pilgrims prayed to satisfy the soul of the inner man, and to assuage the appetite of the outer man they searched the woods for acorns and edible roots, the shores for clams and crabs.

Skeletonlike, these colonists received two ships in 1623 bringing ninety more people. How to feed these mouths, the Pilgrims could not guess. Then for weeks a gentle rain fell. Drooping corn stood upright on revived stalks. By fall Pilgrim bins were filled with a plentiful harvest.

Really to understand what happened there—not only in the Plymouth Colony and the Massachusetts Bay Colony which followed soon afterward—one has to turn to a supremely symbolic figure like Roger Williams, who was born on London's Cow Lane in either 1602 or 1603. (The date cannot be accurately established since the Great Fire of London in 1666 destroyed so many records.) Roger's father was a prosperous merchant-tailor, devoted to the policies of James I; Roger was not. As a lad, he roamed London streets and byways, knowing the city was filled with beggars. The new-fangled horse-drawn carriage, the boy was told, would soon drive the riverboatmen of the Thames out of the transportation business. Pickpockets filled the streets. Across the Thames at Southwark was a questionable settlement of bear pits, taverns, and theaters—no place for a boy to wander alone after sundown.

More damning for Roger was the fact that he wore his hair cut short, the sign of a Puritan. Unlike the long-haired courtiers in satins and velvets and lace ruffles and ostrich plumes, Roger wore dark clothes cut from plain materials. As a Puritan, no matter what the king or the bishops declared, Roger believed that by studying the Bible he must find God in his own heart.

Elizabeth I had scorned such talk. Henry VIII had chained the Bible in the churches so the people could not read it, and the queen, reversing this act, soon regretted her leniency. Puritans, reading the Old Testament, believed that God had endowed them with great rights and grave responsibilities which could not be denied by a sovereign or his bishops or his Parliament.

That dour Scot, James I, virtually frothed at such insolent talk and to prove his point, when Roger was about nine years of age, selected a grim day in March of 1612 to drag Bartholomew Legate (or Leggett), an Essex man, into the Market Square. Legate, in the vigor of his forties, refused to revise his views concerning God and prayer to satisfy those of the king and the bishop of London, so Legate was tied to a stake and "burned to ashes."

If Roger Williams observed this terrible act, it did not shake his conviction. He still cut his hair short. The Puritan church, Saint Sepulchre's, was across the street

from Old Bailey, the debtors' prison, and doubtless
James I would have enjoyed merging them into one. But
Saint Sepulchre's claimed some very famous members,
including Capt. John Smith, explorer and savior of Jamestown, and Sir Edward Coke, who may have possessed
the brightest legal mind of his age. Roger listened atten-
tively to all the sermons, taking them down in a kind of
shorthand he had mastered. Sir Edward watched this
action with intense fascination. Unexpectedly, he approached Roger with an offer. How would the lad like
to earn good wages by recording Coke's legal arguments.

The arrangement worked splendidly. As Parliament's
most prominent Puritan, Sir Edward insisted that man
was endowed by God with certain inalienable rights that
even the king could not revoke. Coke was arrested, as
he must have anticipated. Meanwhile, he arranged for
Roger to continue his education at Charterhouse School
where he could earn a scholarship to Cambridge.

No one should have been surprised when Roger
Williams grew into a militant leader in the Puritan
struggle for separation of church and state. He obtained
the position of chaplain to the household of Sir William
Masham at Oates, Essex. So placid and kind in per-
sonality and so engaging in the delivery of his sermons
was Roger that Sir William would have kept him employed forever. Among those who listened to the young
preacher at Oates were Oliver Cromwell, who one day
would rule England, and John Winthrop, John Cotton,
and Thomas Hooker, all destined to rise to power in New
England.

Among Masham's many enterprises was that of investor in a new London Company seeking to establish a settlement overseas. Suddenly Roger tingled with excitement. Why should he not seize this opportunity to go to America where he would be free to preach as his conscience dictated? His bride of one year readily assented, although she could guess what added hardships she and their newborn daughter must endure. In December of 1630, Roger and his family boarded the *Lyon,* forsaking the Old World for the New.

Charles I solved the problems of settlements in Massachusetts by a royal charter (1629) granting to the Massachusetts Bay Colony all the land from sea to sea in an area three miles south of the Charles River to a point three miles north of the Merrimack River. Two general courts were to run the colony, one composed of stockholders or freemen, and the other of clergymen. Technically, the king's plan laid a basis for representative government in Massachusetts. However, the charter did not stipulate how often the courts should meet. Either independence or chaos could result.

Roger Williams's arrival in America coincided with the beginning of the "Great Migration," which, ending in 1640, brought 16,000 settlers to Massachusetts. His first home was in Boston (called *Shawmut,* "Sweet Waters," by the Indians). Many sad awakenings awaited Roger, who found very little difference between the rule of the Puritans in Boston and the king and his bishops in England. On the theory that the magistrates were the "nursing fathers" of the church, so, naturally, the clergy were the custodians of the court. Only "trouble makers"—such as the Quakers, who were ultimately executed—would complain over so sensible an arrangement.

For Roger to tolerate this dictatorship of clergy and court was impossible. He would not serve in Boston where "the evil of a national church" persisted. For two years he lived as a farmer in Plymouth, a small and isolated community. He was also a trader and missionary among the Indians, studying their languages and customs and winning their approval as a warmhearted friend. Occasionally he preached in the Plymouth church, usually to darkening frowns.

Then Roger received a call to serve the church in Salem (or Jerusalem, as the town was first called). Everyone in Salem seemed to adore Mr. Williams. His sermons, scolding the magistrates for meddling with the freedom of individual congregations, caused heads to nod in agreement.

But some of Mr. Williams's "strange opinions" were too much for the magistrates of Massachusetts Bay to tolerate, as when he declared that "the King had no right to give away lands in America that belonged not to him but to the Indians." Moreover, Roger was accused of being "a user of tobacco." Every small offense was made into a hill of sin, until at last the court decreed "that the said Mr. Williams shall depart out of this jurisdiction within six weeks now next ensuing, which, if he neglect to perform it, shall be lawful for the governor and two of the magistrates to send him to some place out of this jurisdiction, not to return any more without written license from the Court."

In defiance, Roger named his second-born daughter "Freeborn."

But banishment with winter approaching was no joking matter, and Roger was told that as long as he did not "draw others to his opinions" he could remain in Salem. This was like asking the devil to grind down the points on his pitchfork. Soon rumors circulated that Roger not only received visitors in his home but also "preached to them, even of such points as he had been censured for."

Roger heard that an officer was coming for him and that he was to be shipped back to England on a vessel then waiting at Nantasket. "No, thank you," was Roger's mental reply. He arranged with friends for the care of his wife and children, then fled from Salem into the wilderness. Everywhere Indians called him *netop,* their word for "friend."

Spring brought Roger to the shores of the Seekonk River. Wanting badly to have his family join him, Roger was not such a fool as to ignore the wisdom of his Indian friends. Gladly they led Roger to where two freshwater streams (the Moshassuck and the Woonasquatucket) converged, an ideal location for a house. Water gushed from a great spring, and Roger named the location Providence "from the freedom and vacancy of the place and many other providences of the most holy and only wise one."

A wooded hill protected Roger's new dwelling from the north and east winds. Clam beds filled the shores of the rivers. Good meadows stretched westward. A bay teemed with fish. Roger paid the Narraganset, an Algonquian tribe, for the land on which he settled. The chief sachems of the tribe, Miantonomo and Canonicus, called on him.

Roger's relationship with Miantonomo were cordial from the outset. Canonicus was more cautious—or "sour," to use Roger's word—and suspected the English were deliberately spreading a "plague" among his people with himself especially marked for death. Roger, however, won over the old Indian and wrote Governor Winthrop: "At last (through the mercy of the Most High) I not only sweetened his spirit but possessed him that the plague and other sicknesses were alone in the hand of the one God, who made him and us, who being displeased with the English for lying, stealing, idleness and uncleanness (the natives' epidemical sins) smote many thousands of us ourselves with general and late mortalities."

Other families from Salem joined Roger in his new location. The influence of Sir Edward Coke was strong in the democratic spirit of the agreement Roger devised:

We, whose names are here under-written, being desirous to inhabit in the town of Providence, do promise to submit ourselves, in active or passive obedience, to all such orders or agreements as shall be made for public good of the body, in an orderly way, by the major consent of the present inhabitants, master of families, incorporated together in a township, and such others whom they shall admit unto the name, *only in civil things.*

New settlements sprang up at Portsmouth, Newport, and Warwick, and in 1643 Roger journeyed to England to gain a charter for the "Providence Plantations," which was granted in 1644. But Roger found trouble awaiting him at home when William Coddington, who controlled Newport, refused to abide by the charter. Four years later Coddington obtained his own charter and was named governor over all the land he dominated. In 1663, after Roger made a second visit to London, Charles II (the son of Charles I) granted a new charter for "Rhode Island and Providence Plantations." By its terms, "no person . . . at any time" could be molested or punished "for any differences in matters of religion" as long as a person behaved "peaceably and quietly."

But now religion began to bother Roger. Puritanism no longer satisfied him. For a time he was an Anabaptist, then called himself a Seeker who recognized no church as the true one and ministered to no set congregation. Yet as president of the new colony he welcomed followers of all faiths, and although he disagreed with the Quakers, they, too, were welcomed, since almost inevitable death awaited them elsewhere in New England. Even the Puritans who had banished Roger could not resist his charm and referred to him as a "dear fellow."

Today Rhode Island calls itself the "New World's

first free republic." It also can claim the establishment of the oldest houses of three religious groups in North America—one Quaker, one Seventh Day Baptist, one Jewish. But its shining star is Roger Williams, who turned the prejudices of the Massachusetts Pilgrims and Puritans into ideas of tolerance that helped to shape the political structure of the nation into which colonial America emerged.

Chapter 8

THE BIRD FROM HEAVEN
The Dutch, Swedes, and Finns
Invade the New World

Between the English settlements in Virginia and those in
Massachusetts stretched a vast area that lured many nations. It is entirely possible that as early as 1524 Giovanni
da Verrazano, who sailed for the French, first discovered
the Hudson Valley. At about this time a legend sprang
up among the Indians who lived there that one day a
huge bird with white wings had landed in their bay and
then had flown away. Could this white-winged bird,

which they believed would return sometime, have been Verrazano's vessel? For generations father told son about this miracle, but when almost a century passed without the bird reappearing, the legend all but faded from memory.

Meanwhile, the Indians lived in their own easygoing way along the Hudson Valley. Mothers still disappeared into the forests to have their babies where no one could see them. No people ever adored babies more than these Indians, who believed that if a child was mistreated or made to feel unwanted, an evil spirit would carry it to the Land of Lost Souls. To make certain this tragedy would not occur, the child was tied to the ground with corn husks.

Children experienced carefree lives in the Hudson Valley. The warriors taught the boys how to use the bow and arrow, the tomahawk, and the hunting knife. They were taught how to hunt animals, how to spear the great whales that sometimes appeared, how to distinguish between good spirits and bad spirits in the forest. Girls learned which herbs and roots possessed medicinal value, and how to plant and grow vegetables. Children wore shoes made of corn husks, and their winter clothes were sewn from deerskin, elk hide, and beaver pelts.

Old men dressed themselves in coats of turkey feathers. Girls beautified themselves by painting blue and white rings around their eyes. Copper bracelets tinkled on their arms and necks. Bands of snakeskin adorned the braids of their hair. Sometimes "war-parties" set out in long canoes. The warriors wore bonnets of eagle feathers. They liked to hang ringlets of bear claws around their necks. Their faces were streaked with clay every color of the rainbow.

And then one day, almost as though coming out of the mists of memory, the white-winged bird of heaven reappeared. An old legend was revived.

Henry Hudson in his own right was a legend. Already before the year 1609 when he and his ship, the *Half Moon*, startled the Indians of the Hudson Valley, he had made two voyages for a British trading company to test the theory that by sailing north*east* over the north pole instead of north*west* he would find the long-sought passage to the Orient. Instead, at Spitsbergen, a group of islands on the edge of the Arctic Ocean, he enabled his backers to establish whale fisheries that yielded small profits.

Hudson, having worn out his welcome in England, turned to Amsterdam. Here he was given command of the *Half Moon* and a mixed crew, which departed from Holland on April 4, 1609, again in search of a "Northeast Passage." Rounding Norway's North Cape, he entered a sea of floating ice. Bitter cold made the crew mutinous. Hudson reversed his course, and sailed toward the setting sun.

Hudson carried in his pocket a letter from his old friend Capt. John Smith of Jamestown, who argued that an inland passage to the Orient must exist. Foremast gone and sails torn, the *Half Moon* floundered off the Grand Banks of Newfoundland on July 2. Sailing south along the coast, Hudson finally reached Virginia, but discovered little cheer here since Jamestown was just emerging from its starving time and his friend John Smith was in England. French ships fished the waters around him, but Hudson "spoke with none of them." He sailed northward and found safe harbor in mid-July— probably in Maine's Penobscot Bay—but unfriendly Indians added to his troubles with a half-mutinous crew. Hudson sailed away, and after entering Delaware Bay, where shoals scraped the bottom of the *Half Moon,* he again headed northward.

The month now was September. Storms off the New Jersey shore drove him into temporary harbor at Sandy Hook. At last venturing forward, he sailed straight into the river that now bears his name and traveled as far as present-day Albany. If he decided the river was not the northwest passage to the Orient, he certainly was correct. His crew, still bordering on mutiny, may have influenced his decision to beat the winter by sailing straight for Ireland.

Unhappily there is a sad ending to Captain Hudson's career. A British company the following year sent him once more in search of the Northwest Passage. In 1611 a faithless crew fell on Hudson. He was turned loose, with his son and several sick sailors, to drift in a frail boat. Somewhere in icy Hudson Bay, which the captain had discovered, is "his tomb and his monument."

The enterprising Dutch did not forget the New World. Two small trading vessels, the *Little Fox* and the

Little Crane, may have entered in 1611 the bay and river Hudson had discovered. There can be no doubt that after a stormy voyage in 1613 Capt. Adriaen Block reached Manhattan Island (in Indian, *Ma-na-hat-ta* means "Heavenly Land"). His ship burned and he spent the winter there befriended by the Indians. In the spring he built a new ship called the *Onrust* (Restless), and discovered the Housatonic and Connecticut rivers, Rhode Island, and Block Island in voyages during 1614. The reports Block eventually carried home encouraged the Dutch to launch other expeditions to reap the profits the New World promised.

In 1621 the Netherlands government decided that Manhattan should be something more than a petty trading post and founded the Dutch West India Company, endowing it with the powers to make treaties, maintain courts, and employ soldiers. Three years later their ship, the *New Netherlands,* entered the North River with more than one hundred Walloons, chiefly Belgian and French refugees from religious persecution, to start the first permanent colonization in what one day would become the state of New York. Most of them settled at Fort Orange (now Albany), but some stayed on Manhattan and others followed the orange, blue, and white flag to establish settlements deeper in the wilderness. The first girl born on Manhattan Island was Sarah Rapalje, the first white male was Jean Vigue. Four ships arrived bringing more colonists and over one hundred head of cattle in 1626.

That same year the Dutch decided they needed a

director-general to control their possessions in the New World. Peter Minuit, a sly rascal in his own way, was the first choice for this office. Following the Dutch rule to pay for all land occupied, Minuit used beads, buttons, and other trinkets to a value of about twenty-four dollars to purchase Manhattan Island.

At the time the purchase may have seemed no great bargain, for this island, bordered by forests and swamps, was still in large part a dangerous wilderness. Inland, low hills, rich in their growth of oaks and hickories, provided what hope there was for the years ahead. Wolves and panthers still roamed the rock ridges. Occasionally bears lumbered out of the dense thickets to feast on their favorite food, Dutch sheep. Hungry deer trampled vegetable gardens. Up island some Indians still lived in their old wigwams, close to their corn and tobacco fields.

Dutch houses at the lower tip of Manhattan usually possessed two rooms, wooden chimneys, and thatched roofs. Furniture was hewed from rough lumber. Wooden platters and spoons were scraped from the same planks. A village of 200 in 1626 increased to 270 in the next two years. In honor of the chief metropolis of the Dutch Republic, the name was changed first to Fort Amsterdam and then to New Amsterdam.

The United Netherlands bragged of its leadership in the world of art with such masters as Rembrandt van Rijn and Frans Hals. Its University of Leiden was the greatest educational institution in the world. Dutch ships saucily carried brooms at their mastheads to attest to their power to sweep clean the English Channel.

Minuit, falling into an old Dutch habit, treated his colonists as mere servants, totally without rights of owning land, manufacturing, or trading. He permitted them only to do the work of the West India Company, which was to build cabins, warehouses, and mills. The actual earthworks and red cedar palisades of Fort Amsterdam stood on Bowling Green. Two "consolers of the sick" arrived in 1629, and a teacher of the Scriptures in 1630. A year later Minuit was ordered to return home, but the Dutch settlers would hear from him again.

Minuit's successor, Wouter Van Twiller, described as "fat and moon-faced, low of stature and dull of wit," was far shrewder than his critics guessed. When he arrived in 1633, he brought along an accredited clergyman and Adam Roelandsen, the island's first professional schoolteacher. He managed a lively trade in grain with New England, which depended on its fisheries, and with Virginia, which depended on its tobacco, until the vessels he sent back to Holland fairly bulged with valuable peltry. He armed his fort with 104 Dutch troops, erected barracks, and enlarged and strengthened his bastion. Understanding the one thing that made his colonists happiest, Van Twiller built an extremely profitable brewery. Tall windmills were another contribution he made to New Amsterdam. He bought Nutten (Governors) Island and Blackwell's Island to insure his personal future. Apparently the West India Company felt uncomfortable with Van Twiller's "moonlighting." His days thereafter were quickly numbered.

Van Twiller's successor, William Kieft, deserved his

characterization as "little, fussy, fiery and avaricious." The marks of his reign from 1638 to 1647 were a stone tavern near Coenties Slip, the stone church of Saint Nicholas, and a distillery. Hundreds of New Englanders, escaping from the religious intolerance of the Puritans and from Indian savagery, fled to Kieft's protection. But the director-general's unwise policies toward the Indians, added to his greedy imposition of taxes, made the burghers unite against him. Indian troubles increased, and when scores of unarmed and friendly Indians sought refuge on Manhattan Island, they were cruelly massacred.

By 1645 only one hundred people were left in Manhattan and fifteen hundred in the entire Dutch colony. Wisely the States-General of the Netherlands greatly curtailed the West India Company's privileges, thus winning new colonists, until New Amsterdam became the nation's "melting pot" and eighteen nationalities were represented among its population.

That the streets of lower Manhattan appeared to twist unpredictably arose from the fact that a settler could build his home wherever he wished. There were two main roads—the first, Broadway (then called De Heere Straat), led from the Battery to what later would be known as the Old Boston Road; the second, following Pearl Street, led to the road a traveler followed to reach the ferry that crossed to Brooklyn. The path beaten by girls to the pond where they washed clothes was already named Maiden's Path; later it became known as Maiden Lane.

The last director-general of New Amsterdam was Petrus (Peter) Stuyvesant, a veteran of the West Indian wars, who became governor in 1647. He wore a wooden leg fastened on top by a silver band. An extremely short-tempered man, he was arrogant and oppressive. He persecuted dissenters from the Reformed religion like Baptists, Lutherans, and Quakers. He governed the Dutch seaport from a stone *Stadt Huys* (State House), in front of which was constructed a high gallows. By his order the *schout* (mayor) locked the gates of the city at night and opened them in the morning.

Under Stuyvesant New Amsterdam grew into a town of immaculate, gabled Dutch houses. Bowling Green was turned into an area where children danced around the maypole and played other games. In 1658 the first market-house would be established there. Herdsmen, blowing their horns as they arrived in the early morning, summoned other settlers to bring out their cattle to graze. The settlement of Nieuw Haarlem was founded by the peglegged governor. In 1655 the West India Company incorporated New Amsterdam into a city that contained 1,000 citizens and 120 houses. There was even a lawyer.

Cobblestones were used to pave most of the streets, with gutters running down the middle. Gardens brightened the fronts of houses. The fire company owned 250 buckets. Small yellow and black bricks, imported from Holland under orders by Stuyvesant, composed the walls of the homes of the so-called "important."

The city under Stuyvesant was beautiful. Every household had its horse, its pigs and cows, its chickens, its beds of tulips. A carpet of fine white sand covered the parlor floor in the neat houses. Camlet-valanced beds with homespun linen patchwork quilts stood beside iron-bound oaken chests. Precious plate and porcelain ware filled the corner cupboards. Tea tables were surrounded by stiff Russian-leather chairs. The kitchen was the "home room." Here stood the housewife's spinning wheel and the husband's easy chair. The fireplaces were immense, and iron pots hung in them on hooks. Every door had its brass knocker. A fair city lot sold for fifty dollars and a good house rented for twenty dollars a year.

Stuyvesant—Washington Irving called him "Peter the Hardheaded"—was as pleased with his community as with the silver band that fastened his wooden leg. But for Stuyvesant stormy times were brewing.

Twice over a quarter of a century Sweden and Finland, a single kingdom since about 1350, had attempted to plant a colony in the New World and twice had met with disaster—once in a hurricane and again in a sea battle. Doubtless the Swedes held some superstitious belief that the Finns were in some way responsible for both tragedies, since the Swedes were growing quite tired of the Finns by now. They described Finns as "poachers and deserted soldiers," who destroyed the forests and the copper and iron mines, and who "could not pay their debts." Possibly to be rid of as many Finns as they could, the Swedes decided on a third effort at colonization. The South Company (it would change its

name ten times) thus was organized in 1624 to trade in
"Asia, Africa, America," and that part of the world
Magellan had discovered, which was called "Magel-
lancia."

A Netherlander and one-time investor in the Dutch
West India Company, Willem Usselinx, was founder of
the new Swedish venture. After much bickering the
company simply fell apart. So the New Sweden Company was organized, and the time was right for another
Dutchman, Peter Minuit, the former governor of New
Amsterdam, to wander onto the scene. Axel Gustavsson
Oxenstierna, regent for six-year-old Queen Christina,
liked Minuit at once and gave him command of the
expedition's two ships, the *Kalmar Nyckel* (Key of Kalmar) and the *Fogel Grip* (Griffin). The crew was largely
Dutch when on a chilly December day in 1637 Minuit
sailed from Gothenburg. Twenty-two Swedish soldiers
kept close watch over the sailors. The cargo consisted of
supplies to trade with the Indians and wines to sell in
the West Indies.

No account survives of Minuit's voyage before the
March day when he suddenly appeared at Jamestown,
Virginia, "to refresh with wood and water." After ten
days, Minuit headed for Delaware Bay and apparently
made another stop at the Dutch settlement of Zwaanen-
dael, or "Valley of the Swans" (now Lewes). At last he
moved on, coming to the Minquas Kill, near present-day
Wilmington, and in honor of the child-queen renamed
the stream Christina Creek. Here he built a fort.

Indians glided down this waterway in canoes filled with pelts, promising Minuit a rich cargo when he sailed back to Gothenburg. Hammers pounded and axes rang as Fort Christina was constructed. The flag of Sweden whipped in the breezes on the shores of Delaware Bay. Soon an expedition carried the Swedish claim in the New World to the Schuylkill River and then, through purchases from the Indians, up the Delaware River as far as the "Falls" at Trenton, New Jersey.

For a governor of New Sweden a wise choice was Johan Printz, who must be ranked among the best administrators in colonial America. A giant of a man, weighing over four hundred pounds, the Indians renamed him "Big Tub," or "Big Guts." When he mounted a horse, the poor animal's back sagged until Printz's feet touched the ground. He ate and drank in enormous quantities. Some said "his profanity was famous from Massachusetts to Old Point Comfort" in Virginia, but others saw Printz as "a gentleman born and bred, an intrepid soldier, an intelligent, versatile, energetic administrator, and a wily diplomat." A prodigious student who attended four universities in Sweden and Germany, Printz's favorite occupation was war, then considered an honorable profession. He littered with forts the territory Sweden claimed in the New World.

To the Swedes and Finns, colonial America was indebted for the log cabin. Unlike the French, who stood their logs on end (as in a stockade), the Swedes and Finns carefully mortised the corners of their logs so that they could be laid one upon another. Sawed lumber supplied interior fittings, but bricks were imported for the chimneys and fireplaces. The windows were glazed.

Another innovation of the newcomers, the public bathhouse, did not catch on with most colonial Americans. The Swedes and Finns wondered what was wrong with their neighbors. The bathhouse was a large, round log building with a tremendous central fireplace. The bathers undressed and climbed to the balconies built around the walls. There they perspired from the heat of the great fire, and water was poured upon hot stones to raise steam. All the while the bathers switched themselves with bunches of birch twigs. A dip in the river (or a roll in the snow in wintertime) completed the exercises.

The Swedes were a fun-loving people, and Printz built them an alehouse "for singing and folk-dancing." The prosperity of New Sweden in the seventeen years it existed was invariably touch and go. In 1653 Printz had to remind an indifferent Sweden that five and a half years had elapsed since the colony had received a letter from home, even though in a good year they would ship more than two thousand beaver pelts overseas.

Dutch spies were everywhere, watching this invasion of the Swedes and the Finns. In 1645 Andreas Huddle built a fort for the Dutch across the Delaware from the Swedish fort of New Gothenburg, an outpost between Fort Christina and the Schuylkill. Printz fell into a colorful rage—some sources say that he turned "purple"—and tore the ensign from the post of the Dutch West India Company and trampled it in the dust. He reached for his gun to go after Huddle, but was happily restrained.

Printz's outbreaks of rage were understandable. Torrents of rain plagued even peaceful years. In 1645 Sven Wass, on sentry duty at Fort New Gothenburg, fell asleep at his post. A lighted candle fired the fort and spread flames to the magazine: Only a barn escaped the explosion, which could be heard for miles around. Men, women, and children fled for their lives in their nightclothes.

Printz was never the same thereafter. He ordered a certain "Anders the Finn" imprisoned for his debts, and then, acting as "prosecutor, judge, chief witness, and at least the better part of the jury," ordered Anders hanged. No incident could have proved more conclusively that Printz was outliving his usefulness in the New World. In 1653 he left Delaware for home. He lived another ten years before a fall off a horse killed him. A wife and five daughters survived "Big Guts," the Indians' friend.

In his last letter as governor, Johan Printz had given four reasons why the Swedes would fail as colonizers:

1. They [the Dutch] destroy our trade everywhere.

2. They strengthen the savages with guns, shot, and powder, publicly trading with these against the edicts of all Christians.

3. They stir up the savages to attack us, which, but for our prudence, would already have happened.

4. They begin to buy land from the savages within our boundaries, which we had purchased already eight years ago, and have the impudence here and there to erect the seal of the West India Company, calling it theirs; more-

over, they give New Sweden the name of New Netherland, and are not ashamed to build their houses there.

The Dutch came on relentlessly, after Printz's re-
moval, to destroy New Sweden. Their captain sent back
highly vain and optimistic reports, which Stuyvesant
read with reasonable suspicion. The captain, Van Poffen-
burgh (whom Washington Irving preferred to call Pud-
dinghead), erected a fortress on the South River, which
was the Dutch name for the Delaware.

Printz was followed as governor in 1654 by Johan
Claudius Rising, who knew at once that he had inherited
a lost cause. Fort Casimir was "dilapidated." Twenty-
two houses, standing in two rows, constituted the whole
of New Castle. For a time Rising was successful in re-
pairing and controlling the forts along the Delaware.
Then in 1655 a fleet of Dutch ships under the command
of Governor Stuyvesant sailed into Delaware Bay. Rising
knew he had no hope of victory, so completely was he
surrounded by Dutch troops. Luckily the war was soon
over. Fort Casimir and its adjacent town were burned
to the ground; Fort New Gothenburg was reduced to a
shambles. The Dutch became undisputed masters of
New Sweden.

For all they once had been derided as poachers,
debtors, and criminals, the remaining Swedes and Finns
fitted easily into other communities. William Penn, coming later into the Delaware Valley, spoke kindly of them:
"I have yet to see young men more sober and laborious."
Their warm friendship with the Indians became a tradi-

tion. They clung tenaciously to their religious convictions and Gloria Dei, or Old Swedes Church, still stands in Wilmington as a tribute to their devotion.

They did not lack for spunk, either, and when the Hollanders stole a bell from one of their churches, the Swedes and Finns recovered it within two days.

Chapter 9

BRITANNIA RULES!
The Collapse of the Dutch

Officially the English never gave up any claim to the territory surveyed by Cabot in 1497. In frequent letters in the seventeenth century, the English asked, mockingly, "Where is New Netherlands?" New England legislative bodies passed resolutions asking, "Where is there a New Netherland?" The duke of York, Lord High Admiral of England, sent out a fleet which in 1664 appeared before Peter Stuyvesant's town. On his old pegleg with its silver band, Stuyvesant shouted that before he surrended, "I would rather be carried out dead."

Stuyvesant stuck two pistols in his belt, ready to fight the devil. His people and the clergy refused to follow him. They enjoyed little freedom under Dutch rule and could not have much less under the English. The Dutch soldiers surrendered, marching out of their garrison "with their arms, drums beating and colors flying." Actually the duke of York, brother of the British king, Charles II, was engaged in a "treacherous buccaneering attack" to seize all land between the Connecticut and Delaware rivers. In disgust, Stuyvesant moved to his colonial farm on lower Manhattan, where he lived his last eighteen years in peace. Throughout the colonies Dutch names were changed. Thus New Amsterdam became New York.

The first British governor of the colony was Col. Richard Nicolls, a wise and tactful fellow. He spoke Dutch and French as well as he did English. In his four years of rule (1664–68) he reconciled competing factions within the city.

Despite a quick temper, Col. Francis Lovelace, who ruled the city and colony between 1668 and 1672, displayed great energy. He started horse races at Hempstead and bought Staten Island from the Indians. He started the first mail delivery between New York and Boston on a monthly basis. He opened the first merchants' exchange in 1670, where every Friday Dutch and English shopkeepers met at a bridge over the Broad Street Canal.

England and the Netherlands never maintained their

friendships—nor their hostilities—for long, so that it was no surprise when war broke out again. In 1673 a Dutch fleet of twenty-three ships entered New York harbor. Six hundred stout troops landed at the foot of Vesey Street, where they were joined by four hundred burghers. Bravely, step by step, they moved down Broadway toward the English fort, which, to everyone's surprise, surrendered. The orange, white, and blue banner of the Dutch was raised, and the city and harbor, New Jersey and Long Island were ceremoniously reclaimed. New Orange became the name of the conquered city.

But only for a year. Then the Netherlands and Great Britain patched up their differences and New Netherlands was returned to Great Britain. Sir Edmund Andros became governor over all the duke of York's properties in colonial America. That a difficult spirit had entered the New World was almost instantly revealed. Andros filled the canal on Broad Street, moved the tanners to a distant section of Broadway, drove the slaughterhouse into the country, and gave the burghers the exclusive right of bolting (sifting) and exporting flour from the province. Andros's name would reappear in the history of colonial America.

The English were equally contemptuous of the Dutch claim to Connecticut, despite the fact that in 1614 Adriaen Block had sailed up the Connecticut River as far as the Enfield Rapids and traded with the Indians. A Dutch tendency never to develop a territory today that could be conquered on some vague tomorrow allowed twenty years to pass before a trading post and fort were built near present-day Hartford.

Meanwhile the English were not idle. Indian accounts of the fertile soil that could be found in Connecticut aroused their interest. Curiosity led Edward Winslow, governor of Plymouth Colony, to visit the Connecticut Valley in 1633 (by coincidence the year in which a royal grant was given to Lord Say-and-Seale, Lord Brooke, and eleven others to all the land between Narragansett Bay and the Pacific Ocean). Down in New Amsterdam this intelligence outraged Director-General Wouter Van Twiller. A party of Dutchmen hurried to Connecticut, purchased land from the Indians, and nailed the Dutch coat of arms to a tree.

The English were notably unimpressed. The following September, William Holmes brought a small group from Plymouth Colony to Windsor, in the Connecticut Valley. In 1634 John Oldham gathered a band of colonists at Watertown, Massachusetts, and then trudged through the forest to Wethersfield, and next year dissenters from New Town (Cambridge) accompanied John Steel and Thomas Hooker (who only a year before had voted to banish Roger Williams from Salem) to new homes at Hartford, while John Winthrop, Jr., erected a fort at Saybrook. These four settlements along the Connecticut River gave the English a firm foothold there.

England's claim to this country was as good as any the Dutch could advance, and her maps were far superior for those who settled inland communities. Too little credit did anyone give Capt. John Smith for the thoroughness of his explorations beyond Virginia. His unusually fine map, *A Description of New England,* printed in 1616, abounded with the geographical details Smith had acquired in searching for gold and whales, neither of which he found for the London merchants who financed his adventures. Captured by the French, an artist at escape like Smith experienced no great difficulty in achieving a getaway, but even though the settlers at Plymouth had benefited greatly from his books and maps, the Pilgrims drove Smith away when he appeared in their colony. A later edition of his *New England Trials* included an account of his tribulations with the Pilgrims, and many of his earlier narratives found their way into his *Generall Historie of Virginia, New-England and the Summer Isles.* Ultimately, those who read these and others of Captain Smith's steady flow of writings recognized his positive genius.

But the Dutch ignored Smith as stoically as though the captain never had existed, and surely they were yielding nothing to his claims on New England, especially as far as they extended to Connecticut. Indeed, as the Dutch puffed angrily on their clay pipes and contemplated the British intrusion into Windsor, Hartford, and other sections of the Connecticut Valley, the Hollanders planned a brutal revenge. They appealed for help to the Pequots, led by Sassacus, who was dreaded and feared by all Indian tribes east of the Hudson. Two English captains, sailing up the Connecticut River on a trading mission, were murdered. Two girls, working in the fields beside their home in Wethersfield, were carried off as captives, and their parents were brutally beaten to death. John Oldham, who had fathered that settlement, was killed off Block Island. Raids and massacres at Wethersfield and Saybrook continued through the winter of 1636–37.

A general court, representing all the towns in Connecticut, met at Hartford on May 1, 1637. War was declared against the Pequots, and a little army of seventy-seven men was raised under the command of Capt. John Mason, who was a tough old warrior after youthful years of fighting in the Low Countries. The Mohegans and Narragansets brought him guides and allies. Doggedly the square-jawed Mason pursued the Pequots until on May 26 he caught them in a large fort at West Mystic. The circular area covered several acres and contained about seventy wigwams. Chief Sassacus often stopped there.

Dawn had not yet broken. A reconnaissance revealed that the fort contained only two entrances, so Mason decided to divide his army into two parts and attack the openings simultaneously. Quietly the two forces—one under Mason, the other under Lt. Lion Underhill—crept up the hill as the sky lightened. A barking dog awakened an Indian who, looking out, screamed the Pequot word for Englishmen:

"Owanux! Owanux!"

Mason and Underhill poured their forces into the stockade. Sleepy Indians staggered about unaware of what was happening. The English found themselves on

one of the two streets of the fort where stood the wigwams. "We could not but admire," Underhill wrote, "at
the providence of God in it; that soldiers so unexpert in
the use of their arms, should give so complete a volley, as
though the finger of God had touched both match and
flint."

If Underhill was right, then God was engaged in
some pretty devilish work. Indians hid beneath their
bed mats. An Indian, about to take dead aim on Mason,
had his bowstring slashed by a soldier's sword.

"We must burn them!" Mason exclaimed.

The wigwams were fired with a combustible material
that, creating a gas, seemed to make the air burst into
flame. Pequot screams added to the panic. Some,
thoroughly befuddled, ran into the flames. Indian warriors who tried to escape over the walls were shot and
fell back into the fire. The scene of fleeing, shouting
Pequots, mixed with the groans of the wounded and
dying, etched its horror in memory.

In round figures, seven hundred Pequots were "destroyed." Seven escaped. Seven were taken prisoner. Unhappily the war did not end there but required a brutal
battle in a swamp at Fairfield in July before this fearful
business could be called finished. The threat of the
Dutch was ended, but Connecticut's true triumph belonged to Thomas Hooker, founder of Hartford.

Hooker delivered a sermon that Roger Williams
would have enthusiastically applauded. "The choice of
public magistrates," Hooker preached, "belongs unto the

people by God's own allowance. . . . They who have the power to appoint officers and magistrates [also have the power] to set the bounds of the power and place unto which they call them."

Hooker's clear-cut enunciation of the principles of democracy resulted in January of 1639 in the adoption by the neighboring settlements at Windsor, Hartford, and Wethersfield of the Fundamental Orders of Connecticut "to order and dispose of the affairs of the people at all seasons as occasion shall require." Representatives would be selected to elect a governor and magistrates, limit their terms of office, and enforce just taxation.

Clearly breezes of freedom were blowing over Connecticut, even though, upon occasion, they would nurture some odd consequences. The New Haven Colony, founded in April 1638 (two months before an earthquake scared most of its 250 men, women, and children out of their wits) was led by Theophilus Eaton, Edward Hopkins, and the Reverend John Davenport, who adopted probably some of the bluest blue laws ever inflicted upon white Americans. The Reverend Samuel Peters declared that only "an authorized clergyman" could cross a river on a Sunday, no mother could kiss her children on the Sabbath or a fasting day, and "every male shall have his hair cut round according to a cap." No one could read a common prayer or observe Christmas or saints' days. It was illegal to make minced pies, dance, play cards, "or play any instrument of music, except the drum, trumpet, and jew's-harp." And, added the Reverend Peters, "No one shall be a freeman or have a vote, unless he is converted and a member of one of the churches allowed in the dominion." New Haven held itself apart from the other settlements and remained a separate colony until 1664.

John Mason, who had defeated the Pequots, was given two royal grants entitling him to the land between the Merrimack and the Piscataqua rivers. He named the colony's chief seaport Portsmouth since he once had held a lucrative job as governor of England's Portsmouth Castle, and he called the colony New Hampshire after the county in southern Britain where he also had prospered financially. Early settlements were Little Harbour (Rye), Dover, Portsmouth, Exeter, and Hampton. Puritan Massachusetts objected to these Anglican rascals and, picking loopholes in its own charter, claimed the colony in 1639 and governed it for the next forty years.

Actually, there were two Jerseys, under two proprietors, divided roughly by a diagonal line running from Little Egg Harbor to Pensauken Creek above Camden. The Jerseys claimed three explorers—Verrazano (1524); Henry Hudson (1609), who probably investigated without much enthusiasm the land around Newark; and the Dutch navigator Cornelius Mey, who rounded the southern cape, delighted in the play of whales in these waters, and gave his name, if not his spelling, to Cape May. East Jersey, governed by Sir George Carteret, with its capital at Amboy, was well settled by the Dutch, who built neat towns and prosperous farms and even had their own racetrack at Paulus Hook. West Jersey, ruled by Lord

Berkeley, with its capital at Burlington, grew accustomed to the appearance on its southern borders of Swedes, Finns, and Quakers. All were amicably received, even after New Jersey was joined into a single crown colony. Its importance as the link between north and south was never properly appreciated until it became and was called, quite appropriately, the "Cockpit of the Revolution."

In London, a covetous darkness crept into the eyes of Charles II at the growing independence of New England as far south as the Jerseys. Moreover, he resented the sympathy these colonies had displayed toward the enemies of his father. The annexation by Massachusetts of New Hampshire and the territory that one day would become Maine (1820) aroused his ire. The king had given royal charters to Rhode Island and Connecticut only in the hope of curbing the avarice of Massachusetts. Reports of intolerance toward members of the Church of England added to the bitterness of the king's mood. In 1684 he annulled the Massachusetts charter and the colony became a royal possession.

James II, who succeeded Charles in 1685, went even further. He established the Dominion of New England, under the governorship of Sir Edmund Andros, to exercise a proper discipline over Massachusetts, New Hampshire, Plymouth, Connecticut, and Rhode Island. Later New York and a consolidated New Jersey were included in the "Dominion."

Angered at having their charters revoked, the colonies rebelled, and when Andros arrived in Connecticut, demanding its charter, the colonists hid the document in an oak tree. Happily, Parliament supported "The Glorious Revolution," leading to the accession of William and Mary to the throne of England in 1689. The Dominion of New England was a victim of this upheaval. The self-government Andros had tried to destroy returned to Connecticut and Rhode Island. New Jersey was returned to its proprietors. Massachusetts was allowed to keep that region which one day became Maine, and the Plymouth Colony was added to her jurisdiction, but the old Puritan republic was crushed forever when the crown demanded that it practice religious tolerance.

Over the quickly developing English colonies, now settled along the Atlantic coast since the success of Jamestown, blew unrecognized seeds of independence. The result was a strange little civil war in 1676, called Bacon's Rebellion—not a war against England, but the first of many conflicts between British Americans, some of whom believed that they deserved the same rights as the Britons who lived in the motherland across the Atlantic.

Among the first factors that influenced this contest was Governor William Berkeley, who served two good terms as administrator of Virginia. But Berkeley was an "old Royalist," who lost his authority when the Roundheads came into power. During these years Sir William retreated to his plantation at Green Spring, on the road between Williamsburg and Jamestown, where he cultivated two thousand apple, pear, quince, peach, and apricot trees. That the old Royalist sulked through these years of exile there could be no doubt. Ultimately he was restored to power, an irascible, vindictive man.

In Virginia, others were changing as irrevocably as Sir William. Two classes of Virginians reacted to this change. One was the indentured servant, a white person bound to his master until he had worked off the cost of his passage (often exaggerated) to the New World. The indentured servant saw himself as part of a team of oxen, harnessed to the inescapable bondage of a captured Negro slave. Many of these indentured slaves ran away to freedom and a life of their own in the mountains of western Virginia.

Really all Virginians, who did not share in the administration of Sir William, suffered the humiliations of the indentured servant. Once these Virginians had managed their own internal affairs; now they could no longer do so. Taxes increased, the price of tobacco fell off. Sir William refused to act against the increasing number of Indian raids. Why? In view of rising taxes, why did Sir William refuse to call the House of Burgesses into session? Why did he brand any Virginian who questioned his judgment a rogue or a dog?

The time was ripe for a Virginia revolutionist to rise to power, and his name was Nathaniel Bacon. Neither yeoman nor poor man, but the son of a wealthy English countryman, Bacon's prestige was that of a man willing to sacrifice his fortune for what he believed was right. His education at Cambridge and Gray's Inn was finished when at the age of twenty-six he arrived in Virginia. He was a tall man—some said with "a swarthy complexion," others, with "a melancholy eye."

Bacon was appointed to Berkeley's council. But the governor was troubled. The rumors he heard accused Bacon of tending "to atheism," or a belief in no religious sect (and least of all, the Church of England). Meanwhile Bacon established two fine estates, one on the James at Curles Neck, another near Richmond. How could so rich a man be godless?

But Bacon possessed a tendency toward excitability. Against the governor Bacon issued "The Declaration of the People." A list of insufferable abuses followed, ranging from "unjust taxes" to accusations of appointing to "places of judicature scandalous and Ignorant favourites." The governor had assumed "the monopoley of the Beaver Trade . . . protected favoured and Imboldened Indians" without providing "proper meanes of satisfaction for their many Invasions, Murthers and Robberies Committed upon us."

Under these circumstances, Bacon's Rebellion was neither a forecast of the coming American Revolution nor even of the development of the American system of democracy. A fine historian of colonial America, Louis B. Wright, saw the situation as though gazing through a crystal ball: "It was an indication of the spirit of independence engendered among settlers in a region where the acquisition of landed freeholds was easy; it was a declaration that the whole body of freemen would demand the rights which Englishmen were guaranteed under the common law; and it was a warning that the aristocratic system imitative of the English country gentry would have to be adaptable and on guard against political corruption if it hoped to survive."

Bacon's Rebellion was caused by events in 1675. That summer a band of Susquehannocks, driven south by the Senecas, invaded Virginia. They stole a quantity of swine. Settlers under Col. George Mason and Maj. George Brent lost their heads and murdered a party of innocent Susquehannocks, including a chief. The Indians struck back in savage anger. Virginia soil reddened with blood. A larger army of settlers from Maryland and Virginia, now under the command of Col. John Washington, sought a powwow with five sachems. Apparently, for unexplained reasons, these chiefs were killed. For seven weeks Washington sat outside the Indian town, awaiting a battle. Instead, one night the Indians crept away.

The following January seemed riddled with Indian raids. Virginian heads rolled in the dust. The frontier forts were too widely scattered to offer adequate protection, but Governor Berkeley, restored to power, grumbled that forts cost money, as did sending the militia to aid the settlers. Incensed Virginians understood their governor, who was not going to use the colony's bullets to destroy his personal fortune gained from trading for beaver pelts with the Indians. Nathaniel Bacon, who was not one of Sir William's admirers, agreed to take command of an army of three hundred settlers that formed in the upper counties.

Berkeley turned his head aside as though Bacon and his soldiers did not exist. But Nathaniel possessed his hot streak. He arranged with the Occaneechees, a supposedly friendly tribe, for supplies, but when these did not arrive after many days, he suspected Sir William of interfering behind the scenes. Suddenly the governor swept away all pretense. Bacon was declared in rebellion and his army ordered dispersed. Sir William, plainly aware that his popularity was slipping, disbanded the burgesses and called for a new election. To the governor's indignation Bacon was sent by Henrico County to the assembly.

Sir William wondered if wile would work where reprimand failed and offered Bacon a place on the council. The assembly carried on its work amidst these crafty maneuvers. War was declared on the Indians, and young Bacon was selected as commander of the assembly's forces.

This fancy bit of nose-thumbing at the governor stung Sir William, but he pardoned Bacon of previous sins against him as representative of the crown. Setting off for the falls of the James to fight Indians, Bacon grew high-spirited. In a somewhat gloomier mood Berkeley retired to Gloucester, raised his own militia, and once more declared Bacon in rebellion. Since two could play this game, Bacon awaited developments in his headquarters at Middle Plantation (renamed Williamsburg) and branded as traitors the governor and his council members. An armed vessel was sent to capture Sir William at Accomac, a mission that failed through "indiscretion and the juice of the grape."

In exasperation, Bacon revoked the licenses of all tippling houses, inns, and alehouses except at Jamestown and the two ferries that crossed the York, where only cider and beer could be dispensed. Bacon marched off to fight Indians in the marshes along the York, then heard that Berkeley had returned to Jamestown; whereupon, in this almost comic rebellion, Bacon switched his "Small tired Body of Men" around to give combat there.

Reaching Jamestown, Bacon dug trench reinforcements "by the help of the moone light." At daybreak six of Bacon's boys "ran up to the Pallisadees of the Towne and Fired briskly upon the Guard." The Baconites returned unscathed.

Berkeley shouted that no gun should be fired except "upon paine of death." Bacon's big guns now were planted, but for extra protection he seized the wives and females belonging to the governor's cohorts, turning the women to face the royal enemy in a sort of "Bullworkes." Sir William "hurryed away against his owne Will to Accomack," leaving Jamestown to the mercy of its invaders. Bacon decided that the techniques of war compelled him to sack the place. He burned the church, the statehouse (including "the Countryes Records"), and some twelve houses. Bacon occupied Berkeley's home at Green Spring; then, journeying into Gloucester County, he contracted a fatal fever. His death moved an unknown contemporary poet:

Here let him rest, while we this truth report,
He's gone from hence unto a higher court
To plead his cause, where he by this doth know
Whether to Caesar he was friend or foe.

Berkeley had to be twice recalled to London before he departed in May 1677. The statehouse was rebuilt at Jamestown in 1685 but was again destroyed by fire four years later. Discouraged residents decided in 1699 to move the capital to Williamsburg. They were moving—or so they believed—to "a healthier and more convenient place . . . freer from the Annoyance of *Muskettoes.*"

In a sense, a new age (and century) was on the verge of being born—years in which the seed of independence would turn into the seed of liberty.

In 1675, the year before Bacon's Rebellion, King Philip's War exploded upon New England. One of the kindliest and most innocent men in America was responsible for this uprising—unobtrusive, Indian-loving John Eliot.

English-born of a father who owned several parishes in Essex, John was the third of seven children. Cambridge gave him a bachelor of arts degree in 1622, when he was about eighteen years of age. He was, possibly, the best scholar of the classics in the university, and it was when John went to teach in the grammar school at Little Baddow in Essex that he came under the tremendous influence of Thomas Hooker, who converted him to Puritanism.

Thereafter, America beckoned to him. With some of the Winthrop family, he reached Boston aboard the *Lyon* on November 3, 1631. Along with his duties as a teacher, he grew fascinated with the Indians. Always a good grammarian and student of Hebrew, he began studying Indian languages. His long-held ambition to enter the ministry was finally fulfilled. His first preaching to the red*men, at Dorchester Mills in 1646, was in English. He won over a few heathens, and by the summer of the following year was preaching to them in their own language!

Eliot's mission became a sensation in England, where his publication of such titles as *The Day Breaking* led to the formation of several societies that contributed funds for his still greater work—the translation into Indian of the New Testament (1661) and the Old Testament (1663). The cost of this first Bible published in North America was about £1,000, largely contributed by English sympathizers. A small Indian college was established at Cambridge.

Eliot found himself in a pretty fix. His wish, naturally, was to Christianize and civilize all the tribes in New England. At the same time he recognized—and understood—why the Indians disliked living too close to the English. His first town for "praying Indians" was laid out at Natick. By 1674, most authorities say, Eliot had organized fourteen such communities, containing about eleven hundred Christianized Indians. He taught Indians to become their own missionaries, but there were whites who objected to Eliot's fraternizing with the red men. An unyielding Eliot pressed on through New England. In round figures, Eliot and his allies may have converted as many as four thousand "praying Indians."

The great disservice of this work was to disalarm the New Englander of the danger threatening him as year after year he pushed his settlements deeper and deeper into the wilderness. Against the saintliness of an Eliot, were the French and Dutch—at Albany and elsewhere— who supplied the Indians with firearms, knowing the deviltry they were planting.

King Philip knew, too, when as chief he addressed his Wampanoags in Rhode Island. Then he talked to the Nipmucks and the Narragansets. They must save their hunting and fishing rights, Philip said. All that was needed was an incident, and this was soon supplied. A settler in Swansea, Rhode Island, seeing an Indian looting houses, killed the intruder—and King Philip's War followed. That conflict spread its bloodstained trail across Massachusetts and Connecticut. The Indian attacks were savage and without sense. The pattern rarely varied: houses burned, skulls crushed in, women and children carried into a brutal captivity.

The horrible price of this calamity descended upon King Philip. An Indian traitor—bought through a secret alliance between the English and the Naticks and Niantics—led the English to the swamp where Philip was hiding. Not only was the chief killed, but his head was severed and mounted on a pole where it was displayed in Plymouth.

In a sense, colonial America was like the needle of a record caught in a groove. Over and over, at times to the point of near despair, the same discordant melody was repeated.

Chapter 10

BORDER DISPUTE
The Penns and the Calverts

The old admiral was sorely vexed by the son to whom in 1644 he had given his name of William Penn. It did no good to lecture or punish the boy. Not that the lad did not possess brains—he attended Oxford in his early teens. What infuriated the admiral was the fact that at this citadel of English conformity his son, at the age of seventeen, had become a child of the religious dissent then sweeping England. A Quaker! Doubtless for the old admiral's sake Oxford tried to beat a little sense into the youthful William Penn. The university's officials attempted everything—profound argument, simpleminded fines—but neither strategy worked. Only one alternative remained: Oxford expelled the boy in 1662.

The old admiral was as angry as the university. Buckle under, he told William. Or let this disobedience lead you into your own way of life. Adversity made a good Quaker in that age—adversity always nourishes rebellious youngsters.

Young William Penn—the admiral's son—possessed a remarkable intelligence. He did all the things that young men did in those middle 1600s to make their dissent important. He supported the Huguenots in France. He was imprisoned in Ireland and declared that "religion makes me a prisoner of malice, but my own freeman." He returned to England and as a Quaker deliberately insulted the court by appearing with his hat on, an offense against the crown for which he was locked in the Tower of London. The old admiral could not endure such ignominy for his son and, appealing to the duke of York, had William released after nine months of imprisonment.

In 1670—William was now twenty-five years of age— he was back in court. William was happy to duel verbally with the court recorder:

"Under what law am I indicted?"

"The common law," the recorder replied.

"Where is that law?" young Penn asked. "The law which is not in being, far from being common, is no law at all."

The culprit was hurried out of court by a red-faced judge. The jury voted for acquittal. The judge sent the jury back to reconsider their decision, tongue-lashing them severely:

"We shall have a verdict, by the help of God, or you shall starve for it."

William shouted at the departing jurors:

"You are Englishmen; mind your privilege; give not away your right!"

For two days the jury deliberated, receiving no food from an angry judge. On the third day, hungry but unbeaten, the verdict was delivered:

"Not guilty!"

Fines were set upon the jurors which the old admiral paid, perhaps out of a sense of pride in his son. The old admiral tried to speak kindly:

"Son William, if you and your friends keep to your plain way of preaching and living, you will make an end of the priests."

But the old admiral smiled. For all that he called his son "some melancholy thing," he recognized the greatness of William—his rare spirit as a human being, his profound intelligence, his purity of heart.

A dozen years passed. Their toll upon the old admiral was visible to his friends; his death was not unexpected. The claim of his estate against the government for money he had loaned the king amounted to £16,000 ($80,000), a sum that "merrie King Charlie" could not pay. As a compromise, Charles II gave young William Penn a proprietary claim to a colony in the New World, a vast area that stretched westward from the Delaware River between the fortieth and the forty-third degrees of north latitude. In a sentimental mood, the king asked that the colony be named Pennsylvania in honor of the old admiral.

Penn thought deeply about what conditions were indispensible to a good government. In a letter to the Indians, Penn said that he wished "to enjoy it [the colony] with your love and consent." No one knew better than he the injustices other colonists had inflicted upon the Indians, including "the shedding of blood."

"But I am not such a man," Penn continued, "as is well known in my own country. I have great love towards you, and I desire to win and gain your love and friendship by a kind, just and peaceable life, and the people I send are of the same mind, and shall in all things behave themselves accordingly." Indeed, he promised, any Indian charged with a crime would speedily be brought to trial before a jury of six whites and six Indians.

Weeks went into Penn's conscientious planning of a good form of government, which, he believed, should be "a part of religion itself." Three common ideas, he said, must shape a good government: "monarchy, aristocracy and democracy, the rule of one, a few and many." His head hummed with ideas for making government the servant of human decency and dignity.

"If men be good, government cannot be bad," William Penn stated. Good morals made good nations, and all people should join in writing and enforcing the laws. Penn could list many of the laws he wanted in his colony: laws against corruption, fraud, bribery, extortion, and slander. Swearing, lying, drunkenness, duels, bear-baiting, and cockfights he considered sins against God. Nothing should be permitted "which excites the people to rudeness, cruelty, looseness and irreligion."

It was a gala day at New Castle (a town on the Delaware River granted to Penn by the duke of York) when in early November 1682, Penn brought approximately a thousand colonists to American shores. Indians joined whites in the cheers of welcome. Swedes and Dutch, Huguenots and Germans stood elbow to elbow with the English in shouting greetings to their new governor. Almost three thousand had crowded around the landing. The measure of Penn was his promise to the Swedes that they would experience "the best day they ever saw" if they would "serve and obey him." Another mark of the man was the name he planned for his future city—Philadelphia—Greek for "city of brotherly love." The first court was held next day in New Castle. Penn wanted to set his ideas in motion.

As quickly as possible, Penn met with the Indians under an elm at Shackamaxon (part of the future Philadelphia). Chiefs of the Leni Lenapes, the Susquehannocks, and the Shawnees came to work out a "treaty of purchase and amity." Penn never resisted a chance to make a Quaker speech, and his Indian audience heard:

We meet in the broad pathway of good faith and good will; no advantage shall be taken on either side, but all shall be openness and love. I will not call you children; for parents sometimes chide their children too severely; nor brothers, only; for brothers differ. The friendship between me and you I will not compare to a chain; for that might rust, or a falling tree might break. We are the same as if one man's body was divided into two parts; we are all of one flesh and blood.

Penn decided that he would purchase all the land he could cover in a leisurely three-day walk, but after a day and a half he had gone some forty miles and, deciding this was all the land he needed, he called an end to the proceedings. The Indians all but worshiped this man whose religion would not allow him to carry a "hostile weapon." And God appeared also to smile down on him. Two years after Penn's arrival, his "goode greene towne," Philadelphia, contained 357 houses and 2,500 residents as it forged toward becoming the largest city in colonial America. (Boston was second, New York third.) Shipbuilding became an important business, and William Rittenhouse built America's first paper mill on Wissahickon Creek. By 1685 Penn's colony had grown to 7,000 inhabitants.

But not everything was perfect. Penn's claim to the three lower counties of New Castle, Saint Jones, and Deale (which one day would become the state of Delaware) was extremely questionable. Penn appealed for help to the duke of York, who once had turned the key to the lock that imprisoned Penn in the Tower of London. The duke, a sly hand at politics, gave Penn a quitclaim deed relinquishing his legal title to the three lower counties.

Sir George Calvert was knighted by James I in 1617. Sir George's interest in the New World was deep-rooted, first as a member of the East India Company and then of the London Company, which had sent settlers to Virginia. He bought part of Newfoundland in the year the *Mayflower* sailed to America, naming his domain Avalon.

Calvert was a Roman Catholic, as devoted to the Church in Rome as William Penn was to Protestant nonconformity. The risk Sir George ran as a Catholic was great in the England of that age, but when only sixteen days away from death, James I could not forget his old friend and raised him to an Irish peerage that made him baron of Baltimore in the County of Longford. The bishops of London protested. Their persecutions forced the lord of Baltimore to seek asylum in the New World. A pamphlet, *Westward Hoe for Avalon*, told his lordship that here he could expect the freedom suggested by the scent of "red and damask roses." Lord Baltimore twice visited the Avalon section of Newfoundland (where there were not the mermaids the French had promised) but found it too cold and decided instead "to plant and dwell" in Virginia. An interesting dialogue occurred between Virginia's Governor Harvey and Lord Baltimore:

Q. Will you take the oath which we all have taken?
A. I cannot with good conscience.
Q. Then you must leave with the first ship hence to England.

Lord Baltimore had no intention of leaving. He settled for a grant giving him the country north and east of the Potomac River and embracing Chesapeake Bay. This colony he named Maryland in honor of Queen Henrietta Maria. The new colony was defined as extending along each side of Chesapeake Bay from the fortieth degree of latitude north of the Potomac and westward along the line of the river. The claim obviously overlapped that of Penn. Lord Baltimore died before the great seal could be affixed to his claim, which on June 20, 1632, passed on to his son Cecil. Cecil carried on his father's convictions of religious toleration—not that he had much choice in the matter, for the two hundred settlers who were aboard the *Ark* and the *Dove* when in 1634 Cecil sailed into the sparkling waters of Chesapeake Bay were not quite evenly divided between Protestants and the outnumbered Catholics. The Yaocomico Indians traded for axes, hatchets, farm tools, and bolts of cloth an entire village, complete with wigwams, so that the Marylanders had only to build a statehouse to give their colony its capital city of St. Mary's. Although as a name for his colony Cecil would have preferred Crescentia, meaning "Land of Increase," political shrewdness led him not to press the issue.

But Cecil would not budge on his pledge of religious freedom. Those persecuted by Puritans in New England and Anglicans in Virginia found ready welcome in Maryland. When in 1642 Thomas Gerard, a Catholic member of the council, seized the key and Bible from a Protestant chapel, Gerard was fined five hundred pounds of tobacco to be sold for the support of the first Protestant minister to settle in the colony. England was outraged by the laws passed in Maryland and shipped them back to the colony, disapproved. Stoically, Marylanders returned the laws under which they chose to live.

No one raged more loudly over this colony than the Archbishop of Canterbury. To him Maryland had become a "pest-house of iniquity" which could only be cured by "an established support of a Protestant ministry." Maryland's Toleration Act of 1649 must have added to the archbishop's fury. This legislation imposed severe punishment for molesting the religion of any "believer in Christ." In protecting all religious sects, the act also stigmatized as guilty of a misdemeanor anyone who derided a fellow citizen as a "Heretick, Schismatick, Idolator, Puritan, Presbyterian, Independent, Popish Priest, Jesuit, Jesuited Papist, Lutheran, Calvinist, Anabaptist, Brownist, Antimonian, Barrowist, Roundhead [or] Separatist." One day the celebrated Quaker George Fox preached to members of the legislature, justices of the peace, and an assemblage of Indian chieftains. He stood on the shore of Chesapeake Bay, an innate kindness lighting his face. His audience rested against trees whose leaves rustled in a gentle wind. Fox's voice sounded musically and his congregation listened as though entranced.

Religious freedom was not Cecil's only source of troubles. A conflict with the inhabitants of Kent Island, a trading post that William Claiborne had established in 1631, threatened to become a sprightly little war before the governor of Virginia intervened and soothed ruffled feelings. Around 1654 a party of Puritans seized control of Maryland on the grounds that freedom of conscience did not belong to the "Popery or prelacy," but this uprising was quickly quelled. Then in 1689 the "Glorious Revolution" in England brought William and Mary to the throne, and for a quarter of a century Catholic Maryland was run as a crown colony with its capital moved to Annapolis. Not until 1715, when the fifth Lord Baltimore publicly renounced "the Romish errors," was the colony returned to the descendants of the original proprietors.

For generations Maryland and Pennsylvania bickered over boundaries as a result of their overlapping grants. The situation became more involved as the years passed on. Claims and counterclaims complicated the issue, and tempers boiled. Nine local surveyors with a rude chain spent three years on a survey that satisfied no one.

It was not until a few short years before the American Revolution that two gentlemen from England, the astronomer Charles Mason and the surveyor Jeremiah Dixon, fashioned the famous line that bears their names, and settled the dispute as far as it ever could be settled.

As for the avarice of William Penn's heirs, there was no solution but a mounting hatred which, in time, cost many lives. Even today Pennsylvanians are so ashamed of the "Walking Purchase" that they would like to forget it.

The tract of land at the junction of the Delaware and

Lehigh rivers, which the Indians had sold to William Penn, had been decided on the forty miles which, in a leisurely manner, the Quaker had walked in a day and a half. But now a new Penn, Thomas, had taken over the claim, and he pointed out to the Indians that the original contract had specified that William Penn had a claim to all the land he could walk in *three* days. The Indians, with darkening frowns, admitted these conditions of their contract, and thought they would lose another forty miles.

But never had the Indians expected what the heirs of William Penn now did. A prize of £5 and 500 acres was offered to the man who could walk the longest distance in the remaining day and a half. The "greatest" walkers in the colony were sought—Edward Marshall, a noted hunter; James Yeates, known for his speed afoot; and the sturdily constructed Solomon Jennings, who looked like a giant.

The walk began on September 19, 1737, beneath a chestnut tree near the present site of Wrightstown. To judge that the affair was properly conducted, a number of suspicious Indians accompanied the officials and a group of white men, some of whom carried refreshments.

The race began as a farce and ended as one. Soon the white men increased their pace until they were almost running. Angrily Indian voices cried out:

"Cheaters! Cheaters!"

Many of the Indians refused to go farther.

For twenty miles from the start spectators lined the course of the march. One remembered:

First came Yeates, stepping as light as a feather, accompanied by several persons on horseback; after him, but out of sight, came Jennings with a strong, steady step, and yet, far behind, came Marshall, apparently careless, swinging a hatchet to balance the motion of his body, and eating a biscuit.

Bets were placed on the winner. Yeates was the favorite. Jennings dropped out the first day. Marshall came on doggedly.

By nightfall the walkers reached the north side of Blue Mountain, where they slept. At sunrise they began anew.

At Durham Creek, at the foot of the mountain, Yeates knew that his legs had failed and he collapsed in the water. Marshall dragged him out. Yeates turned blurred eyes toward the sky, destined to be blind for the remaining three days of his life.

Marshall pushed on to a spur of Second or Broad Mountain. Some say he had covered 60 miles, others that his distance from the starting point was 66½ miles. Jennings, broken in health, died within a very few years. Marshall lived to be ninety.

But the real losers of the race were the Pennsylvanians. Never again would the Delaware Indians trust them.

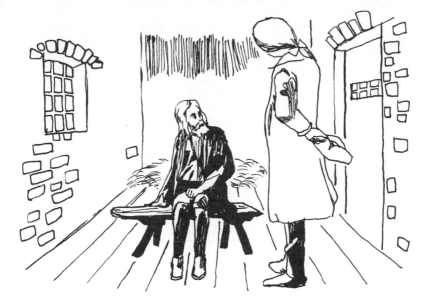

Chapter 11

THE WAR OF JENKINS' EAR
Oglethorpe Captures Georgia

Both the Spanish (near Winyah Bay) and the French (near Port Royal Sound) had failed to secure permanent settlements in the Carolinas, a region toward which the British now cast covetous eyes. In 1629 Charles I granted a claim to Sir Robert Heath, the king's attorney general, to all the territory from "sea to sea" between the thirty-first and thirty-sixth parallels—a land called "Carolina" after the Latin word *Carolus,* the source of the king's own name. For the next thirty-one years no serious effort was made to establish a settlement. In 1663, with Charles II restored to the throne, Carolina was granted to eight lords proprietors, and a few years later a royal commission explored the region.

The first permanent settlement, planted in the Albemarle Sound area in 1670 and intended to encourage the development of large plantations, suffered an uneven decade. In 1680, determined to find a more healthful environment, the proprietors moved to the area between the Ashley and Cooper rivers and renamed the place Charles Town. As the southernmost English outpost against the Spanish and French, Charles Town's population grew steadily, due largely to an influx of English from Barbados and the arrival of persecuted French Protestants. An amiable Irishman, James Moore, who filled many official posts and combined the happy faculties of being both a devout churchman and a gentleman with an eye for quick profits, was especially helpful in stimulating the colony's growth.

Good money was made from rice and indigo. A lively trade in deerskins was developed. A free library, a theater, and a musical society reflected the colony's cultural growth. Yet there were also troubles while such notorious pirates as Blackbeard, Stede Bonnet, and Anne Bonney prowled the Carolina coast. A vicious Indian war, led by the Yamasees, threatened to destroy the colony in 1715–16. The settlers rallied as muskets blazed and tomahawks whirled. Charles Town was saved.

Just so many tears could be shed over the Lost Colony at Roanoke, which, somewhat incorrectly, would be called "the birthplace of English America." Sir Walter Raleigh spent the equivalent of $200,000 and his political reputation in trying to establish an enduring colony in North Carolina, but all he could ever show the Old World was proof that the New World contained three phenomena—tobacco, the white potato, and Indian corn.

John White was the true colonizer of North Carolina, but war between England and Spain delayed his return to Roanoke. The mysterious word "Croatoan," which he found carved on a tree whence his colony had strayed, may have indicated, according to A *Dictionary of Americanisms*, "a group of several thousand people evidently of mixed Indian and white blood, found in eastern N.C., esp[ecially] in Robeson County."

When in 1729 seven of the proprietors sold back to the king their grants in "The Land of the Charles," North Carolina and South Carolina became separate colonies. Aristocratic Virginians were prone to sneer at North Carolina as "Rogue's Harbor," for few were its schools and churches. When North Carolina became a royal colony, old settlers still spoke with awe of the frightful war fought with the Tuscarora Indians in 1711. They could point out hundreds of mounds where white victims of that conflict lay buried. But now that the king had taken charge, North Carolina flourished. Under five royal governors the colony's population in forty-five years increased from 30,000 to 265,000.

And these were good settlers, too—planter aristocracy, largely English and Scottish Highlanders who took over the Cape Fear, Neuse, and Albemarle regions. Germans and Scottish-Irish, it was said, transformed the Piedmont section into a "prolongation of Pennsylvania," for good farmers they were by instinct.

England still needed one colony to protect its hold upon the Atlantic seacoast above Florida and to act as a buffer against the Spanish. Doubtless it was part of English genius that for a reason no one ever could suspect the right man was ready at the right moment.

No colonizer in colonial America excelled James Edward Oglethorpe in nobility of mind, heart, and spirit. His mother, who came from Ireland, lived in the palace of Charles II, where she met Theophilus Oglethorpe, a soldier in the king's army. So distinguished was his military performance that the monarch awarded him with a fine London home and the title of Sir Theophilus. Here James was born on December 22, 1696, the youngest of seven children. Some authorities say he was endowed from infancy "with the abiding loyalty to the Crown, the military and parliamentary family tradition, strong moral courage, and a high purpose."

Sir Theophilus died when James was only five, and so the lad truly was raised by his oldest brother to respect the family motto of "Never Give Up." James remembered the baskets of food his mother had had him carry to the poor. The miserable lives these unfortunates suffered made a deep impression on James. At his mother's insistence he attended Eton, where he was named to the Queen's Guard. James enjoyed his fancy uniform as he rode stiffly beside the carriage whenever the queen went traveling. He was only seventeen when he enrolled at Oxford, where he spent two years.

As though following in his father's footsteps, James joined Prince Eugene of Austria in a war against the Turks and so well pleased his leader that the young man was made a staff officer. In that age many believed that the Turks intended to overrun all of Europe. The battle at Belgrade was typical of the viciousness of this conflict. Thousands on both sides were killed. Where the bullets buzzed the thickest, young Oglethorpe could be seen waving his sword and rallying his men to turn back the Turks.

Obviously the Lord had other work for James, since he escaped without a scratch. He returned to England in 1719, and "from his rural retreat" won a seat in Parliament from the district of Haslemere, which his father and two older brothers had represented for thirty-two years. In this time when the Industrial Revolution was struggling to gain a firm foothold, James advocated naval preparedness and the expansion of imperial commerce. His progressive ideas have led many to compare him to Edmund Burke, Benjamin Franklin, and Thomas Jefferson.

Oglethorpe was shocked when he visited a friend, Robert Castell, who was incarcerated in a debtors' prison. He was appalled by the dreadful conditions under which these poor, indebted wretches lived. Castell slept on a bed of straw. Vermin covered the floor and walls of the cramped room which he shared with a number of other prisoners. The food that was shoved to him through a little opening in the door was sometimes nothing more than a soup into which maggots had fallen.

Before Oglethorpe could pay off Castell's debts, that poor fellow died of smallpox. James thereupon turned his attention to the injustice of the debtors' laws. Another of his crusades stemmed from his bitter hatred of slavery and the evils of impressment. This led to his writing a pamphlet, *The Sailor's Advocate*, that was published in eight editions.

But in and out of government, wherever he could corral a friend, James talked about the debtors' prisons and finally won from Parliament a committee to investigate these institutions. The prison where Robert Castell had died seemed far more merciful in its treatment of its inmates than the other debtors' jails in England. To the twelve English colonies now stretched along the Atlantic seacoast, Oglethorpe suggested the addition of a thirteenth—a colony for the poor.

Georgia—one day to be called the "Empire State of the South"—did not have a happy beginning. In the years before Oglethorpe appeared, Creeks and Cherokees bathed in Warm Springs, which, medicine men said, was stoked by fires under the earth to cure whatever illnesses afflicted these aborigines. Apparently, judging by ceremonial mounds, a number of Indian civilizations had flourished and expired there long before the appearance of the Creeks and the Cherokees. In 1540 Hernando de

Soto had met only hostility there, forcing him onward to his tomb somewhere in the depths of the Mississippi. The Spaniards tried to claim the land in 1565 but were driven off with ferocity by the Indians. For 150 years the territory remained practically unknown to whites.

Then noble James Edward Oglethorpe arrived on February 13, 1733. His ship, the *Anne,* brought some 125 colonists who settled about eighteen miles above the mouth of the Savannah River. Debtors could not sail without the permission of those to whom they owed money, and likely not more than a dozen received this grant. The remainder of Oglethorpe's 125 colonists were poor people—carpenters and blacksmiths, farmers and bricklayers—who had to prove their good character to their leader before they could board the *Anne.* Oglethorpe had many false visions, among them the dream that silkworms, living on the leaves of mulberry trees, could supply through their cocoons enough silk to support a colony.

Tomochichi, a chief of the Yamacraws, an outlawed tribe of the Creeks, took at once to Oglethorpe. He gave James a deed to a site on a bluff of the Savannah River. Oglethorpe planned diligently to give a new and better life to his colonists, and especially to the persecuted Protestants (principally Lutherans and Moravians). A ship bearing forty Jews likewise was welcomed. The colony, named Georgia after George II, who gave Oglethorpe a grant "for settling poor persons of London," claimed after eight years a population of 2,500. The grant was for twenty-one years.

All manner of difficulties would afflict Oglethorpe. The French and Spaniards, infiltrating through Florida to build fortifications, were constant enemies.

Oglethorpe returned to England in 1734 to apologize to his backers for his delinquency in answering their correspondence. In England he won important legislation prohibiting in Georgia the sale of rum and the introduction of Negro slavery. A licensing system for peaceful negotiations with the Indians was established.

When Oglethorpe returned to Georgia in 1736, he was delighted with how Savannah had grown during his absence and how well the settlement had followed his original plan. Now almost two hundred houses stood in squares of four streets, each facing onto a park where the colonists could rest under live oaks and magnolia trees. Relationships with the Indians, based on fair trade and the education of red-skinned youngsters in reading and writing, grew friendlier as time went by (the fact that the ninety-year-old chief's wife was part Scottish probably also helped the situation).

In the following months Oglethorpe must have been a very busy man, for Parliament had appropriated large sums for him to build twenty forts. So intent was Oglethorpe on the need for defense in this buffer colony against the Spanish in Florida that, aboard his first ship to America, he had drilled his settlers in the use of arms. With growing suspicion the Spaniards watched these forts spread throughout Georgia, and when one arose on the banks of the Saint Johns River, only thirty-five miles from Saint Augustine, Spanish patience exploded. Did not Oglethorpe understand that he was an intruder on land that belonged to Spain? Oglethorpe laughed in the faces of his enemies. The land, he declared, belonged to the Indians and had been fairly deeded to the English.

Still, to be on the safe side, Oglethorpe hurried home to London and this time returned with six hundred soldiers. Many of these troops quickly grew tired of the loneliness and hardships of wilderness life. Oglethorpe sneered at any soldier who could not withstand the rigors of his profession. The dissidents mutinied, and several attempts were made on Oglethorpe's life before the disloyal elements were wiped out.

The Spanish tried in vain to woo the Indians from the English. But Spain never failed for new malicious ideas, and she now arrogantly limited the number of ships England could send to supply her American colonies. In 1731 the British brig *Rebecca,* on a return voyage after a trading trip to the West Indies, was intercepted by a Spanish guard ship. Many outrages were committed against the English, including cutting off the ear of Robert Jenkins, the *Rebecca's* master mariner.

With the ear in a jar, Jenkins stormed into Parliament and related the atrocities he and his crew had suffered. England declared war on Spain in 1739, and the conflict became known popularly as the "War of Jenkins' Ear." In America the end came with an attack by sea and land in 1743 on Saint Augustine. Although Oglethorpe tried to trick his opponents by dividing his army into small bands, each with a drummer, and marching them in and out of the trees of the forest to create the impression that he possessed a truly numerous force, the attack on Saint Augustine was a farce and a failure.

Even before this fiasco, however, James Oglethorpe's popularity was slipping. His storekeeper made unwarranted expenditures, and Oglethorpe's laws were called too harsh. Again he was ordered back to London to stand trial before a court-martial, but the charges against him were judged "frivolous . . . and without foundation." In 1752 he and fellow trustees surrendered their charters and Georgia became a royal province.

Still, it was just as well that Oglethorpe's colonizing days in Georgia had ended. The law prohibiting the sale of liquor was abolished, and in 1749 slavery was introduced into the colony. In the next five years Georgia would import 7,800 Negroes. Its white population was about 10,000. Farming, cattle raising, and horse breeding were the foundations of its growing economy.

Oglethorpe's last years were brightened only by a second marriage and his inclusion in the literary circles of Samuel Johnson, James Boswell, Oliver Goldsmith, Horace Walpole, and Edmund Burke. Oglethorpe died in 1785. His high place in the history of two continents cannot be denied; some imperial philanthropists may have equaled him, but none was his superior.

Chapter 12

FREEDOM'S FERMENT
Triumph and Tribulation

The settlement of colonial America was an astonishing accomplishment. That the New World should become a mixture of saints and rogues was not exceptional: the Old World was cluttered with both. That superstition, in the form of witchcraft, should become temporarily planted among the Puritans of Massachusetts was not so surprising as we now view it, for such beliefs had existed among Europeans of all levels of intelligence for hun-

147

dreds of years. Cotton Mather, whose writings and sermons were largely responsible for transplanting this wickedness into the New World, considered himself both God-fearing and honorable. He was not surprised that witches appeared in Massachusetts, but very likely he was troubled that so few of them were found. After all, he knew that a large number of witches had been hanged in England.

Torture was not uncommon in obtaining confessions, and at least one man was crushed to death under the weight of the stones piled on him in an effort to make him admit he was a witch. A special court presided over by Sir William Phips was established to condemn these "accused wretches." The testimony sounded as if those brought to "justice" were speaking under a hypnotic spell. A segment of the testimony given by Mary Lacey can stand as a good example of what these proceedings in New England were like:

Q. Do you acknowledge now you are a witch?
A. Yes.
Q. How long have you been a witch?
A. Not above a week.
Q. Did the Devil appear to you?
A. Yes.
Q. In what shape?
A. In the shape of a horse.
Q. What did he say to you?
A. He bid me not to be afraid of any thing, and he would not bring me out; but he has proved a liar from the beginning.

Later the questioning grew sharper:

Q. What meetings have you been at, at the village?
A. I was once there and Richard Carrier rode with me on a pole, and the Devil carried us.
Q. Did not some speak to you to afflict the people there?
A. Yes, the Devil. . . .
Q. What shape was the Devil in then?
A. He was a black man, and had a high crowned hat.

Young women fell into fits and declared that they were suffering as though stuck with pins. All the time poor, demented Mary Lacey was being examined, another woman, obviously a "victim," writhed on the floor in excruciating pain. Another witness at a similar trial testified: "In the time of this prisoner's trial, one Susanna Sheldon in open court had her hands unaccountably tied together with a wheel band, so fast that without cutting it could not be loosed. It was done by a specter, and the sufferer affirmed it was the prisoner's."

Hundreds of persons were accused of such bedevilment, and altogether nineteen men and women, branded as witches in 1692, were executed by Sir William's special court. Then, suddenly, public sentiment turned against such actions. The legislature called for a public fast so that penance could be done for these wrongs.

Massachusetts, however, was also a leader in *good* acts. Harvard College, the first of the nine institutions of higher learning in colonial America, was established in

1636, and six years later the general council decreed that every mother and father must teach their children how to read and how to practice at least one trade. In another five years the court decided that all communities containing fifty families or more must maintain schools to instruct their children in reading and writing. Towns of a hundred families or more must maintain schools capable of preparing their students for Harvard.

For the boys and girls of colonial America the important year was 1690, when an English printer and rhymester, Benjamin Harris, reaching Boston, published the *New England Primer*, of which approximately two million copies were sold during the next century. Any child today who has lisped "Now I lay me down to sleep" has gained something from the *Primer*. Harris, a Calvinist who moved his shop to "the Sign of the Bible, overagainst the Blew Anchor," knew exactly what parents wanted their children to read. His *Primer* contained "Godly Admonitions," "The Dutiful Child's Promises," "An Alphabet of Lessons," "Texts of Scriptures," and a "Rhymed Alphabet" which contained such entrancing information as:

> N   *Noah did view*
> *The old World and new.*

The English rhymester also published John Cotton's *Spiritual Milk for Boston Babes*, and it was small wonder, even though Boston's first bookstore had opened in 1652, that within eight years Benjamin Harris had become America's foremost publisher and bookseller.

Farms in colonial America changed as the years passed. To harvests of beans, corn, and pumpkins the English added cabbages, turnips, onions, carrots, and parsnips; the Dutch brought beets, spinach, endive, leeks, parsley, and dill; the Germans contributed asparagus, and the Swedes, peaches. Wheat and cereals became other products of colonial farms in the mid-1650s, especially in the Connecticut Valley.

In Falling Creek, Virginia, in 1619, America's first ironworks stimulated the founding of other ironworks as far north as Saugus and Braintree, Massachusetts. In another quarter of a century, iron nails replaced wooden pegs in building dwellings and furniture. Blacksmith shops grew like toadstools in every village. Chains and plows, axheads and scythe blades, hoes and pitchforks became a common sight in farmyards. Along the dusty roads the two-wheel cart could be seen.

The industrial growth of colonial America took many forms:

In 1623 Maine's first sawmill began operating near York, and the same year New Hampshire established a saltworks near Piscataqua.

In 1626 the Dutch in New Amsterdam gave America its first flour mill, and three years later in Massachusetts the first brick kiln was built (Salem) and the first tannery established (Lynn).

In 1634 a water mill for grinding corn existed at Dorchester; a glass factory increased Salem's industries in 1641, which was two years before skilled Yorkshire cloth workers, arriving in Rodney, Massachusetts, opened a wool mill.

In 1624, a ship carpenter, arriving in Plymouth, opened horizons seldom dreamed of for the New World, resulting in 1641 in the launching of a ship of three hundred tons (almost twice the size of the *Mayflower*). In another twenty-five years, it was said, not only were thirteen hundred boats fishing regularly off the Grand Banks of Newfoundland, but another three hundred were engaged in trading voyages to almost every port in the world.

Once, single file, Indians had beaten their tracks through the forests—trails such as Roger Williams had followed, escaping from Salem—but a white man's road became a rod wide (16½ feet). Post riders could carry mail over such roads for whatever currency a colony would accept—beaver skins in New York, wool in Rhode Island, rice in South Carolina, tobacco in Virginia. In 1662, in Boston, a silversmith named John Hull created the first coin, the "pine tree" shilling. The silver was crude, the coin about the size of a half-dollar. It competed with the Spanish dollar, which could be broken into eight pieces and thus created our modern slang of "two bits" for a quarter of a dollar.

Statistics, although dull, are important. By 1650 the growing population of English in America had reached 52,000 and, with the Dutch added to their ranks, would reach 85,000 in another ten years.

To picture as idyllic the existence or character of every colonist who crossed the Atlantic would be the sheerest nonsense. True, the thousands of Germans who fled from the Palatinate and other parts of the Rhineland made industrious, prosperous farmers of whom Pennsylvania could be justly proud. But the hard life of the colonies broke down whatever character some settlers ever had possessed and made them more the victims than the beneficiaries of the New World.

Whereas almost everything written by William Byrd, a prominent plantation owner in Virginia, had to be taken as an example of sophisticated humor, his travels into the backwoods of North Carolina doubtless carried strong elements of truth. Of this "Lubberland"—a lubber is a grasshopper—Byrd wrote caustically:

The men, for their parts, just like the Indians, impose all the work on the poor women. They make their wives rise out of their beds early in the morning, at the same time that they lie and snore, till the sun has risen one-third of his course and dispersed all the unwholesome damps. Then, after stretching and yawning for half an hour, they light their pipes, and, under the protection of a cloud of smoke, venture out into the open air; ... [where] they stand leaning with both their arms upon the cornfield fence, and gravely consider whether they had best go and take a small heat at the hoe, but generally find reasons to put it off till another time. Thus they loiter away their lives, like Solomon's sluggard, with their arms across, and at the winding up of the year scarcely have bread to eat. To speak the truth, it is a thorough aversion to labor that makes people file off to North Carolina, where plenty and a warm sun confirm them in their disposition to laziness for their whole lives.

Surely no one could question the honor (or gentle
humor) of Sarah Kemble Knight, a Boston schoolmistress
who determined soon after the turn of the eighteenth
century to travel to New York City. Even to this woman
of worldliness the journey over roads cluttered with
thieves and cutthroats was harrowing. Stubbornly Miss
Knight pressed on. Sleep at night was rare, even in the
better type inns. One night the schoolmistress tossed in
bed, awakened by the rising voices of some "town topers"
over whether the Indians had named their country Narragansett because of a brier that grew there or because
it was subject to extremes of heat in summer and of cold
in winter. Exasperated, the sleepless Miss Knight
reached for her diary:

> ... They kept calling for t'other gill, which, while they
> were swallowing, was some intermission; but, presently,
> like oil to fire, increased the flame. I set my candle on a
> chest by the bedside, and sitting up, fell to my old way
> of composing my resentments, in the following manner:
>> *I ask thy aid, O potent Rum!*
>> *To charm these wrangling topers dumb.*
>> *Thou hast their giddy brains possest—*
>> *The man confounded with the beast—*
>> *And I, poor I, can get no rest.*
>> *Intoxicate them with thy fumes:*
>> *O still their tongues till morning comes!*

In New Haven, "at a merchant's house," she met a
country fellow "with his alfogeos [cheeks] full of tobacco;
for they seldom loose their cud, but keep chewing and

spitting as long as their eyes are open." Often she went
to bed supperless, unable to swallow the innkeeper's
food; but in New Rochelle, "a French town," she managed to secure a good breakfast, and "on the strength of
that about an hour before sunset got to York."

In *An Account of Two Voyages to New England,*
John Josselyn wrote about the men of Maine. Actually a
colony of Massachusetts, Maine was little more than the
primeval forest it had been since the moon and sun had
first illuminated the earth. A rough people lived there,
mostly fishermen and planters, who were woefully over-
charged for the supplies sent them from Massachusetts—
shoes, goods for clothing, commodities of every sort.
Josselyn described these half-civilized folk:

> They have a custom of taking tobacco, sleeping at
> noon, sitting long at meals, sometimes four times in a
> day, and now and then drinking a dram of the bottle ex-
> traordinarily: the smoking of tobacco, if moderately
> used, refresheth the weary much, and so doth sleep.
> *A traveler five hours doth crave*
> *To sleep, a student seven will have,*
> *And nine sleeps every idle knave.*

A Maine physician declared that an inhabitant needed
but three draughts at a meal—one for need, one for
pleasure, one for sleep. Their food, generally, was not
well cooked when melted snow had to be used. The fish
caught by the Maine settlers went to many ports—Lisbon,
Bilbao, Bordeaux, Marseilles, Toulon, Rochelle, Rouen,
among other cities. The cheapest grade of fish was put

off at the "Carib Islands, Barbadoes, Jamaica, etc., who feed their Negroes with it." Fishing was hard work, particularly when it came to sorting out and salting down the catch. And what did the Maine settler have to show for his labor? Josselyn continued:

> ... When the day of payment comes, they may justly complain of their costly sin of drunkenness, for their shares will do no more than pay the reckoning; if they save a kentle or two to buy shoes and stockings, shirts, and waistcoats with, 'tis well; otherwise they must enter into the merchant's books for such things as they stand in need of, becoming thereby the merchant's slaves, and when it riseth to a big sum are constrained to mortgage their plantation if they have any; the merchant when the time is expired is sure to seize upon their plantation and stock of cattle, turning them out of house and home, poor creatures, to look out for a new habitation in some remote place, where they begin the world again. The lavish planters have the same fate, partaking with them in the like bad husbandry.

But an even worse fate awaited the wild men of Maine.

Chapter 13

DISASTER AND HOPE
A Back Door to Empire

When in 1493 the Pope decreed that the New World should be divided between Portugal and Spain, the French, like most nations in Europe, simply laughed aloud. Few edicts ever have claimed less significance. Indeed, the voyage that Jacques Cartier made in 1534, while searching for the Northwest Passage, brought another type of white explorer into the New World.

Cartier was a man of splendid instincts. For two

weeks he voyaged up the Saint Lawrence River until he came to a fine harbor near the present site of Quebec. In three small boats he left his main fleet and, in early October, landed near present-day Montreal. He received a joyous welcome from the Indians, and Cartier was the kind of man who could enjoy singing and dancing.

Next day, down a well-beaten road between fringes of oaks, over ground strewn with acorns and past fields "full of grain," the French moved to the fortified Indian town of Hochelaga. Timber frames covered with bark distinguished its houses, about fifty in number. In each house was a large central fire around which the family lived.

Cartier met the king of these people, Agohanna, whose authority was demonstrated by the band of red porcupine quills around his head. The Frenchman saw that the chief was a sick old man with weakened arms and legs. Cartier massaged the sore limbs gently, affectionately, and Agohanna, feeling better, suddenly placed his red band upon Cartier's head.

All the sick in the tribe—the blind, the lame, the aged whose eyelids hung so low as to cover their vision—came forward for Cartier to cure them. With some he succeeded, and with some others he did not. But Cartier, who came as a healer and not as a conqueror, was an unusual explorer. He read the Gospel of Saint John to the Indians.

"All these poor people," wrote a contemporary, "kept a great silence and were marvelously good hearers, looking up to heaven and making the same ceremonies that they saw us make." Afterward Cartier gave tin plates to the women, knives to the men, hatchets to the chiefs. Small rings, scattered on the ground, made the children cry out in delight as they scrambled for them. The Indians heaped food before him—rancid food, unfortunately, such as no Frenchman could eat. But Cartier excused himself graciously and left the New World as a hero.

As much could not be said for Samuel de Champlain, who also sailed for France. The first voyage of this old sea dog to the North American colonies was made in 1603. He explored the Saint Lawrence, as Cartier had done three quarters of a century before, and was warmly welcomed by the Indians when he reached the rapids above Montreal. He explored the North American coast southward to Cape Cod, and in the summer of 1608 at Quebec founded the first successful white settlement in Canada.

Unhappily, Champlain enjoyed meddling in frontier warfare. In the spring of 1609, when the Algonquins and Hurons took to the warpath against the Iroquois, the Frenchman could not mind his own business. Champlain, crossing the lake that now bears his name, attacked the Iroquois in a battle near present-day Ticonderoga. With an old-fashioned matchlock gun, which could be loaded with four bullets, he killed two Iroquois and wounded a third. The enemy, awed by this extraordinary performance, "lost courage and took to flight."

Champlain congratulated himself, quite falsely. For

at least the next century—and perhaps longer—the Iroquois and their allies hated the French.

Unable to gain empire through the front door—that is, through successful settlement along the Atlantic seaboard—the French tried the back door. The manner in which the explorers led missionaries up the Saint Marys River to Sault Sainte Marie, which connected with lakes Superior and Huron, is usually written about in romantic terms. In like manner tales are told of how Jesuit missions were founded at Saint Ignace on Mackinac Island and at Green Bay, where Wisconsin's Fox River empties into Lake Michigan. Idyllic language customarily relates the feats of Jacques Marquette, a priest who had served at both Sault Sainte Marie and Saint Ignace, and who, with Louis Joliet, a mapmaker of Quebec, explored the Mississippi as far south as Arkansas.

Truth supported all these stories but failed to reveal the real objective of the French, which was to destroy all English settlements. Depending on what Indian and Canadian allies they could obtain, should they launch a war against New England or New York? Their contempt for the English dwelling in either region was restricted by their respect for the pro-English Indian warriors who roamed the forests of the Hudson Valley.

So the choice was New England, which could be approached through Maine, that so-called "protectorate" of the Massachusetts Bay Colony. Ferocious Indians abounded there—the subtribes of the Abenakis, who reputedly added the word "wigwam" to the English language, and those large bands of warring red men who gave their names to such great rivers as the Kennebec, Penobscot, and the Androscoggin. In May 1702, Governor Joseph Dudley of Massachusetts journeyed through this uncivilized country of wolves, lynx, and cougars to sign a peace treaty at Casco. Two of the principal chiefs, called Captain Samuel and Captain Bomazeen, admitted that the Jesuits had tried to excite them against the English, but they were "firm as mountains." Dudley, aware that the Indians had loaded their muskets, kept a safe distance and luckily departed before two hundred French and Indians arrived "resolved to seize the governor, council and gentlemen, and then to sacrifice the inhabitants at pleasure."

The French governor of Canada, M. de Vaudreuil, was a rascal by any definition, and so were some of the Jesuits, who were making a nice private profit from trading in furs. The Treaty of Casco was a meaningless act. The white settlements of Maine were confined principally to the southwestern corner of that territory in a scraggly line from Kittery to Casco. What were called "forts" were nothing more than houses with projecting roofs with holes through which a settler could shoot at Indians who tried to burn down the white man's homes. Until Harvard graduates some years later penetrated this wilderness, the people were without religion and were lazy and almost constantly drunk, so that as targets they were like birds sleeping on a fence railing.

When the French and Indians attacked, the slaughter was terrible. Villages were burned, and the men and aged were murdered. Women and children were carried off as captives (but if a baby insisted on crying too frequently hot coals were tossed into the infant's mouth). No one dared walk the road, for any thicket could conceal an ambush of Indians with hatchets raised.

Winter was a time when Vaudreuil was likely to send a war party from Canada. The village of Deerfield, in the Connecticut Valley, which in 1704 marked the extreme northwestern frontier of Massachusetts, was typical of the target the French governor preferred.

Snow came early and piled high that winter, giving residents of Deerfield a feeling of security. Mothers sang lullabies to their babies. Sentries napped by their outdoor fires. A town watchman, half asleep, never gave the alarm as the Indians and Frenchmen attacked. They came, more than 250 strong. The snowbanks made it easy for the enemy to climb over the fortified walls surrounding Deerfield. Quickly they scattered through the settlement, carrying torches to light up the deviltry in which they were engaged. They kicked open doors. They pulled the triggers of guns and slashed with their knives. Clubs crashed down upon the heads of children. The night glowed with the flames of burning cabins.

Furiously, the citizens of Deerfield fought back (never trusting an Indian or Frenchman as long as they lived). The lucky ones, pleading for mercy, were carried off to captivity in Canada. Some hid in dark corners. With firebrands Indians raced through the dwellings, ate whatever food they could find, stole any article of clothing or furniture they fancied. And yet a Mrs. Ruth Catlin, watching a wounded Frenchmen carried into her house, ordered him laid upon the floor and given a drink of water.

A shocked neighbor cried: "How can you do that for your enemy?"

Mrs. Catlin replied: "If thine enemy hunger, feed him. If he thirst, give him drink."

Her house was not burned.

The depredations of the French, thus begun, would continue for almost half a century. Freedom was never part of their scheme, the same omission that the Dutch had made. They wanted not a New World but an Old World transplanted across the Atlantic.

In years to come the English-speaking colonies would produce settlers who became world famous.

—In the birth on January 17, 1706, of Benjamin Franklin, philosopher, printer, and diplomat.

—In the birth sometime in 1725 of George Mason, cranky landholder who put the rights of conscience above the rights of property as father of the American Bill of Rights.

—In the birth on February 22, 1732, of George Washington, statesman and soldier.

—In the birth on April 13, 1743, of Thomas Jefferson, who, living high in the Blue Mountains of Virginia, found that, like an eagle, his mind could soar toward those intellectual heights William Penn had once expressed:

"If men be good, the government cannot be bad."

INDEX

PRINTED IN U.S.A